CFP EXAM
Calculation Workbook

Coventry House Publishing

CONTENTS

SECTION 1

FINANCIAL PLANNING PRINCIPLES

QUESTIONS

1. Liz wants to deposit an amount today that will last for 5 years. She needs to withdraw $1,300 at the beginning of each 6-month period, and she'll earn 8% compounded semi-annually on her investments. How much does she need to deposit to achieve her goal?

   A. $8,250.17
   B. $9,364.01
   C. $10,965.93
   D. $11,374.26

2. Mary would like to receive the equivalent of $35,000 in today's dollars at the beginning of each year for the next 7 years. She assumes that inflation will average 3%, and she can earn a 7% compound annual rate of return on her investments. How much does Mary need to invest today in order to achieve her goal?

   A. $217,039.87
   B. $219,172.72
   C. $221,361.56
   D. $224,611.80

3. Jacob wants to start his own business in 4 years. He needs to accumulate $150,000 in today's dollars to fund the start-up costs. He assumes that inflation will average 5%, and he can earn an 8% compound annual rate of return on his investments. What serial payment should Jacob invest at the end of the first year to achieve his goal?

   A. $34,175.13
   B. $35,083.65
   C. $36,472.82
   D. $37,727.11

4. John deposited $425 into his money market account at the end of each month for the past 4 years. His account is now worth $24,915. If interest was compounded monthly, what was the average annual compound return that he earned over the 4-year period?

   A. 9.9%
   B. 10.3%
   C. 10.7%
   D. 11.1%

5. What is the IRR of a 1-year investment in a REIT, if $200 is invested at the beginning of each month? Assume the REIT's end of year value is $2,500.

   A. 6.33%
   B. 7.52%
   C. 8.96%
   D. 9.02%

6. Ryan wants to save $65,000 for a down payment on a new motor home in 4 years. He can invest $1,200 at the beginning of each month, and he expects to earn 8% compounded monthly on his investments. How much will Ryan have saved in 4 years?

   A. $66,454.35
   B. $67,129.34
   C. $68,070.70
   D. $69,310.18

7. Jim would like to save $60,000 for his son's college education. His son will begin college in 12 years. Assume that Jim can invest $15,000 now, and $500 at the end of each 3-month period. What annual rate of return is required for Jim to achieve his goal?

   A. 4.52%
   B. 4.79%
   C. 4.86%
   D. 5.03%

8. Christine's investment of $3,400,000 produces the following cash flows:

   Year 1: $2,100,000
   Year 2: $2,200,000
   Year 3: $1,600,000

   If the discount rate is 7%, what is the net present value (NPV)?

   A. $1,670,749.25
   B. $1,790,258.62
   C. $1,920,102.46
   D. $1,980,638.10

9. Rachel takes out a $170,000, 15-year fixed loan at 5.50%. How much interest will she pay by the end of the loan period?

   A. $80,028
   B. $84,514
   C. $89,216
   D. $93,073

10. William purchased an investment for $750. He kept the investment for 6 years before selling it. If the internal rate of return for the 6-year period was 7%, what was the final selling price?

   A. $1,125.55
   B. $1,137.70
   C. $1,148.91
   D. $1,156.65

11. Jane has been investing $4,125 at the end of each year for the past 18 years. Assuming that she has earned 6.35% compounded annually on her investments, she has accumulated a total of:

A. $128,482.90.
B. $131,794.07.
C. $134,638.44.
D. $137,120.73.

12. Sam purchased an investment for $41,210. He expects it will increase in value at a rate of 7.25% compounded annually for the next 5 years. If his expectations are correct, how much will his investment be worth at the end of the fifth year?

A. $51,365.62
B. $54,599.34
C. $55,182.29
D. $58,477.54

13. Beth wants to accumulate $105,000 in 8.5 years to fund her child's college education. She expects to earn an annual rate of 12.5% compounded quarterly. How much does she need to invest today to achieve her goal?

A. $36,882.01
B. $37,543.98
C. $38,793.35
D. $39,181.69

14. Tony's investment of $200 produced the following cash flows:

Year 1: $80
Year 2: $110
Year 3: $120

If the required rate of return is 12%, what is the net present value (NPV)?

A. $44.53
B. $46.18
C. $48.34
D. $50.27

15. Megan expects to receive $1,250,000 from an irrevocable trust in 17 years. If the trust is earning an annual rate of 9% compounded quarterly, its current value is:

A. $275,298.90.
B. $277,346.01.
C. $280,321.32.
D. $283,902.87.

16. Carl has been investing $3,200 at the end of each 6-month period to accumulate funds for his daughter's college tuition. The funds are earning an annual rate of 5% compounded semiannually. When Carl's daughter begins college in 6 years, how much will the account be worth?

    A. $40,763.45
    B. $42,526.78
    C. $43,992.15
    D. $44,145.77

17. Angela purchased an investment for $950. She kept the investment for 5 years and then sold it for $1,300. What was the investment's internal rate of return (IRR)?

    A. 6.5%
    B. 7.8%
    C. 8.1%
    D. 8.5%

18. Alpha Corp. provides the following data regarding cash flows for a capital project:

Year	0	1	2	3	4	5
Cash flow	–$32,000	$19,000	$6,000	$12,000	$14,000	$3,000

    If the required rate of return is 6%, the net present value (NPV) is:

    A. $13,813.96.
    B. $14,671.02.
    C. $15,092.77.
    D. $16,302.25.

19. Jeff sued his former employer and won a judgment that provides him $3,000 at the end of each 6-month period for the next 7 years. If the account that holds his settlement earns an average annual rate of 5% compounded semiannually, how much was the employer initially required to pay Jeff?

    A. $33,170.16
    B. $35,072.74
    C. $37,517.24
    D. $39,839.07

The following information relates to questions 20 – 21.
Beta Corporation is investing $900,000 in a new production facility. The present value of the future after-tax cash flows is estimated to be $950,000. Beta Corporation currently has 80,000 outstanding shares of stock with a current market price of $14.00 per share.

20. What will be the value of Beta Corporation after the investment?

    A. $1,120,000
    B. $1,170,000
    C. $1,190,000
    D. $1,204,000

21. What will be the value of Beta Corporation's share price after the investment?

    A. $14.63
    B. $15.26
    C. $15.89
    D. $16,12

22. Assuming semiannual compounding, what is the current price of a zero-coupon bond with a $1,000 face value, a yield-to-maturity of 7.98%, and 4 years until maturity?

    A. $710.27
    B. $719.78
    C. $725.53
    D. $731.25

23. A bond has a market price of $920 and a face value of $1,000. If the bond pays a 12% semiannual coupon payment and matures in 4 years, what is the bond's yield-to-maturity?

    A. 14.72%
    B. 15.19%
    C. 16.37%
    D. 17.68%

24. If comparable bonds are yielding 11.2%, what is the current price of a $1,000 face value bond that pays a 9% semiannual coupon payment and matures in 7 years?

    A. $819.14
    B. $840.88
    C. $895.17
    D. $908.04

25. Jessica invests $4,000 today with the expectation that she will receive $9,000 in 5 years. If interest is compounded weekly, what is the average annual rate of return that Jessica will earn?

    A. 13.38%
    B. 14.12%
    C. 15.85%
    D. 16.24%

26. What is the IRR of a bond with a current price of $965, a face value of $1,000, a 7% semiannual coupon, and 3 years until maturity?

    A. 6.47%
    B. 7.10%
    C. 8.34%
    D. 9.56%

27. Assuming semiannual compounding, what is the IRR of a zero-coupon bond with a $1,000 face value, a current market price of $840, and 3 years until maturity?

A. 5.72%
B. 5.90%
C. 6.03%
D. 6.12%

28. If comparable bonds are yielding 8.8%, what is the intrinsic value of a bond with a $1,000 face value, a 6% semiannual coupon, and 5 years until maturity?

A. $888.68
B. $900.97
C. $912.33
D. $922.35

29. Melinda's annual gross income is $50,000. If she pays $15,000 in annual income tax, then her total consumer debt payments, such as credit cards and auto loans, should not exceed _____ per month.

A. $583.33
B. $816.67
C. $833.33
D. $1,166.67

30. Victoria's annual gross income is $100,000. If she pays $25,000 in annual income tax, then her total housing debt costs, including principal, interest, taxes, and insurance, should not exceed _____ per month.

A. $1,166.67
B. $1,750.00
C. $2,333.33
D. $3,000.00

31. Adam's annual gross income is $80,000. If he pays $20,000 in annual income tax, then his total debt payments should not exceed _____ per month.

A. $1,866.67
B. $2,200.33
C. $2,400.00
D. $2,600.67

32. Sigma Lending Company's underwriting requirements specify a maximum housing debt-to-income ratio of 28%. If the applicant discloses annual earnings of $75,000, what is the maximum monthly PITI payment the mortgage company will accept?

A. $1,750
B. $1,825
C. $6,250
D. $21,000

33. George earns an annual income of $95,000, and he would like to purchase a new house. He expects to make a 20% down payment and finance the remaining amount. If the mortgage lender will provide a loan equal to 2.5 times annual income, what is the maximum house that George can afford to purchase?

    A. $190,000
    B. $237,500
    C. $284,425
    D. $296,875

34. Cameron assumed the loan for a property that he recently acquired. If loan interest payable for the current month is $610, and the interest rate is 4.75%, then the principal balance is:

    A. $148,390.65.
    B. $154,106.56.
    C. $158,126.60.
    D. $164,975.50.

35. Henry's loan balance is $300,000 and carries a 4% interest rate. If monthly payments are $1,500, then how much will the principal be reduced by the second payment?

    A. $500
    B. $502
    C. $504
    D. $506

36. Randy assumed the loan for a parcel of land that he recently acquired. If the loan balance is $230,000 and requires an interest payment of $4,600 each quarter, the annual interest rate is:

    A. 7.0%.
    B. 7.5%.
    C. 8.0%.
    D. 8.5%.

37. Nicole owns a warehouse with a current value of $185,000. Justin owns a building with a current value of $350,000 and a $40,000 loan balance. If Nicole assumes the loan, a fair trade would require:

    A. Nicole to pay $125,000 cash.
    B. Nicole to pay $225,000 cash.
    C. Justin to pay $125,000 cash.
    D. Justin to pay $225,000 cash.

38. Evangeline's mortgage carries an interest rate of 4.25%. If the interest payable for the current month is $1,243.66, then what was the mortgage balance at the beginning of the month?

    A. $351,147.75
    B. $353,425.78
    C. $357,981.80
    D. $359,610.37

39. Mark obtained a 20-year loan with a beginning balance of $247,350. The interest rate is 4.65% and the monthly payment is $1,584.96. How much total interest will be paid if the loan runs to maturity?

    A. $127,478.47
    B. $133,040.40
    C. $138,582.70
    D. $143,019.34

40. Ashley purchased a home and obtained an interest-only loan with a balance of $300,000 and a 6% interest rate. The term of the loan is 30 years, including the interest-only period of 7 years. How much interest will Ashley have paid after the first 3 months of the loan?

    A. $4,239.31
    B. $4,434.83
    C. $4,486.23
    D. $4,500.00

41. Dan acquired a 15-year loan in the amount of $250,000. If the interest rate is 4.8%, what will be the principal balance after the first monthly payment of $1,951.04?

    A. $248,912.14
    B. $249,048.96
    C. $249,224.36
    D. $249,308.28

The following information relates to questions 42 – 43.
Laurie obtained a 20-year loan with a current balance of $140,000. The interest rate on the loan is 6% and the monthly payment is $1,003.00.

42. What will be the interest payment in the first month?

    A. $694
    B. $700
    C. $703
    D. $706

43. What will be the principal payment in the first month?

    A. $303
    B. $304
    C. $306
    D. $308

44. Jose obtained a 30-year mortgage with a balance of $60,000. If the interest rate is 5.25%, the first month's interest payment will be:

    A. $258.25.
    B. $260.00.
    C. $262.50.
    D. $264.50.

45. Carol has a loan with a current balance of $613,564. The monthly payment is $3,849, and the house was recently appraised for $902,300. What is the loan-to-value ratio?

    A. 62%
    B. 64%
    C. 66%
    D. 68%

46. Alex obtained a loan in the amount of $592,300. If the annual interest rate is 4.625%, then how much interest will he owe in the first year?

    A. $2,282.82
    B. $19,210.83
    C. $26,482.34
    D. $27,393.88

47. Maria obtained a 30-year mortgage in the amount of $340,000. The interest rate is 5.5% and the monthly payment is $1,930.48. How much total interest will be paid over the life of the mortgage?

    A. $340,000.00
    B. $354,972.80
    C. $356,270.73
    D. $358,389.34

48. If the first month's interest payment on a loan is $612.50, and the interest rate is 7.5%, the loan balance is:

    A. $97,000.
    B. $98,000.
    C. $99,000.
    D. $100,000.

The following information relates to questions 49 – 52.
Karen purchased a house for $160,000 and obtained a mortgage in the amount of $120,000. The interest rate on the mortgage is 5% and the monthly payment is $700.

49. How much interest will be paid in the first year?

    A. $500
    B. $6,000
    C. $8,424
    D. $17,550

50. How much interest will be paid in the first month?

    A. $0
    B. $200
    C. $500
    D. $700

51. How much principal will be paid in the first month?

    A. $0
    B. $200
    C. $500
    D. $700

52. What will be the mortgage balance after the first month's payment?

    A. $119,600
    B. $119,800
    C. $119,850
    D. $119,900

53. If Bill borrows $224,000 and pays $5,600 semiannually in interest, then the annual interest rate on the loan is:

    A. 3.5%.
    B. 4.0%.
    C. 4.5%.
    D. 5.0%.

The following information relates to questions 54 – 55.
Barbara has a 30-year mortgage with a current balance of $240,000 and an interest rate of 5.5%. Her house was recently appraised for $320,000.

54. What is the amount of equity in Barbara's house?

    A. $80,000
    B. $185,000
    C. $275,000
    D. $460,000

55. What is Barbara's debt-to-equity ratio?

    A. 1:4
    B. 1:3
    C. 3:1
    D. 4:1

56. Gamma Corporation sold products to customers on April 30, 2016 for a total price of $85,000. Payment is due in 60 days. The total cost of the products was $67,000. What is the net change in Gamma Corporation's total assets on April 30, 2016?

    A. $0
    B. $18,000
    C. $67,000
    D. $103,000

57. Delta Corporation reports the following information for the fiscal year (in millions):

Revenue	$6,115
Expenses	$3,770
Beginning retained earnings	$510
Liabilities at year-end	$985
Contributed capital at year-end	$440
Dividends	$0
Effective tax rate	35%

What is the value of Delta Corporation's total assets at year-end?

    A. $1,935 million
    B. $3,260 million
    C. $4,280 million
    D. $8,050 million

58. Theta Corporation provides the following information on their year-end financial statement:

Common stock	$205,000
Retained earnings	$230,000
Long-term debt	$615,000
Effective tax rate	35%

What is Theta Corporation's debt-to-capital ratio?

    A. 0.59
    B. 0.73
    C. 0.75
    D. 0.77

59. In 2016, Kappa Manufacturing Company purchased and installed a new machine. The company reported the following costs:

Purchase price	$65,000
Freight delivery	$6,500
Installation	$2,300
Testing	$1,900
Repainting the factory	$800

What is the total cost of the machine to be shown on the Kappa Manufacturing Company's balance sheet?

A. $69,200
B. $73,800
C. $75,700
D. $76,500

60. Omikron Corporation reports the following information at its annual shareholder meeting:

Liabilities at year-end	$500,000
Contributed capital at year-end	$100,000
Beginning retained earnings	$150,000
Revenue during the year	$300,000
Expenses during the year	$200,000
Dividends paid during the year	$50,000

What is the value of Omikron Corporation's total assets at year-end?

A. $800,000
B. $900,000
C. $1,300,000
D. $1,350,000

61. Lambda Holding Company reports the following information for the fiscal year (in millions):

Distributions to owners	$195
Net income	$350
Beginning retained earnings	$625

What is Lambda Holding Company's ending retained earnings?

A. $155 million
B. $470 million
C. $780 million
D. $970 million

62. Omega Corporation has an effective tax rate of 25%, retained earnings of $2.8 million, and contributed capital of $1.3 million. What is the owners' equity for Omega Corporation?

A. $1.5 million
B. $2.1 million
C. $4.1 million
D. $5.1 million

63. Beta Inc. provides the following information for the fiscal year:

Net income	$660,000
Number of shares outstanding	40,000
Price per share	$19.50
Total assets	$3,250,000
Total liabilities	$2,980,000

What is Beta Inc.'s book value?

A. $78,000
B. $192,000
C. $270,000
D. $930,000

64. Alpha Inc. provides the following information in its annual report (in millions):

Shareholders' equity	$57,500
Fixed assets	$48,200
Total debt	$44,100
Revenue	$66,900
Expenses	$53,800

What is Alpha Inc.'s debt-to-capital ratio?

A. 43.4%
B. 57.3%
C. 65.9%
D. 70.8%

65. Helen's rental property produces annual gross income of $36,000. Expenses associated with the property are $12,000 per year. If the capitalization rate is 14%, what is the market value of her property?

A. $85,714.29
B. $171,428.57
C. $205,904.12
D. $257,142.86

66. Epsilon Real Estate Corporation estimates that an apartment building, if fully leased, would generate gross monthly income of $55,000. If the company applies a 7% vacancy rate and uses a 10% capitalization rate, what is the current value of the apartment building?

A. $6,138,000
B. $6,147,000
C. $6,290,000
D. $6,310,000

67. The seller has agreed to pay 1.5 points to the mortgage company to help the buyer obtain a mortgage. The house was listed for $725,000 and is being sold for $695,000. If the buyer will pay 15% in cash and borrow the remaining amount, the seller will owe _____ to the lender for points.

A. $8,861.25
B. $9,243.75
C. $10,425.00
D. $10,875.00

68. Jerry is obtaining a mortgage with closing costs equal to 1.75 discount points. If the property is valued at $220,000, and the mortgage is 85% of the property's value, then how much will Jerry pay in closing costs?

A. $3,080.90
B. $3,120.40
C. $3,190.25
D. $3,272.50

69. If real GDP declined last quarter, how many more consecutive quarters of decline would be needed to be classified as an economic recession?

A. 1 quarter
B. 2 quarters
C. 3 quarters
D. 4 quarters

70. If real GDP declined the last 3 quarters, how many more consecutive quarters of decline would be needed to be classified as an economic depression?

A. 1 quarter
B. 2 quarters
C. 3 quarters
D. 4 quarters

71. When calculating gross domestic product (GDP), all but which of the following variables are paired with the correct description?

A. C = Personal consumption
B. I = Issuance of government bonds
C. G = Government spending
D. E = Net exports

72. A research analyst provides the following economic information for Country X:

Category	Amount ($ billions)
Consumption	11.4
Government spending	3.3
Capital consumption allowance	5.0
Gross private domestic investment	6.2
Imports	2.9
Exports	1.8

What is the gross domestic product of Country X?

A. $17.9 billion
B. $18.6 billion
C. $19.8 billion
D. $24.8 billion

73. Sigma Publishing Corporation has provided the following information regarding the cost of producing a textbook:

Stage of Production	Sales Value ($)
1. Production materials	
Paper	$1.50
Ink	$0.25
Binding supplies	$1.10
2. Assembling each book	$2.00
3. Wholesale price for booksellers	$6.00
4. Retail price	$12.00

According to the value-added method, what is the contribution of textbook production to GDP?

A. $6.00
B. $12.00
C. $13.10
D. $20.85

74. David had five credit cards in his wallet when it was stolen. The credit cards were fraudulently used before he could report them missing. He provides the following amounts that were charged against each card.

Card 1: $50
Card 2: $800
Card 3: $475
Card 4: $30
Card 5: $450

What is David's total liability for these transactions?

A. $0
B. $50
C. $230
D. $1,805

75. Ray would like to help his grandson pay for his college education by funding a 529 plan. Assuming that Ray has not made previous contributions to a 529 plan, what is the maximum contribution that he can make in a single year if the gift tax annual exclusion is $15,000?

A. $15,000
B. $30,000
C. $75,000
D. $100,000

ANSWER KEY

1. C
Begin Mode
PMT = $1,300
n = 5 × 2 = 10
i = 8 / 2 = 4
FV = 0
PV = ? = $10,965.93

2. B
Begin Mode
PMT = $35,000
n = 7
i = [(1.07 / 1.03) − 1] × 100 = 3.8835
FV = 0
PV = ? = $219,172.72

3. D
FV = $150,000
n = 4
i = [(1.08 / 1.05) − 1] × 100 = 2.8571
PV = 0
PMT = ? = $35,930.58 × 1.05 = $37,727.11

4. A
PMT = −$425
n = 4 × 12 = 48
FV = $24,915
PV = 0
i = ? = 0.8266 × 12 = 9.9

5. B
Begin Mode
FV = $2,500
n = 1 × 12 = 12
PMT = −$200
PV = 0
i = ? = 0.6264 × 12 = 7.52

6. C
Begin Mode
PMT = −$1,200
n = 4 × 12 = 48
i = 8 / 12 = 0.6667
PV = 0
FV = ? = $68,070.70

7. D
PV = -$15,000
n = 12 × 4 = 48
PMT = -$500
FV = $60,000
i = ? = 1.2573 × 4 = 5.03

8. B

$$NPV = CF_0 + \frac{CF_1}{(1 + r)^1} + \frac{CF_2}{(1 + r)^2} + \frac{CF_3}{(1 + r)^3}$$

$$NPV = -\$3,400,000 + \frac{\$2,100,000}{(1.07)^1} + \frac{\$2,200,000}{(1.07)^2} + \frac{\$1,600,000}{(1.07)^3}$$

NPV = -$3,400,000 + $1,962,616.82 + $1,921,565.20 + $1,306,076.60 = $1,790,258.62

9. A
n = 15 × 12 = 180
i = 5.5 / 12 = 0.4583
PV = -$170,000
FV = 0
PMT = ? = $1,389.04
($1,389.04 × 180) – $170,000 (principal) = $80,028

10. A
PV = -$750
n = 6
i = 7
PMT = 0
FV = ? = $1,125.55

11. B
PMT = -$4,125
n = 18
i = 6.35
PV = 0
FV = ? = $131,794.07

12. D
PV = -$41,210
n = 5
i = 7.25
PMT = 0
FV = ? = $58,477.54

13. A
FV = $105,000
n = 8.5 × 4 = 34
i = 12.5 / 4 = 3.125
PMT = 0
PV = ? = $36,882.01

14. A

$$NPV = CF_0 + \frac{CF_1}{(1 + IRR)^1} + \frac{CF_2}{(1 + IRR)^2} + \frac{CF_3}{(1 + IRR)^3}$$

$$NPV = -\$200 + \frac{\$80}{(1.12)^1} + \frac{\$110}{(1.12)^2} + \frac{\$120}{(1.12)^3}$$

NPV = -$200 + $71.43 + $87.69 + $85.41 = $44.53

15. A
FV = $1,250,000
n = 17 × 4 = 68
i = 9 / 4 = 2.25
PMT = 0
PV = ? = $275,298.90

16. D
PMT = -$3,200
n = 6 × 2 = 12
i = 5 / 2 = 2.5
PV = 0
FV = ? = $44,145.77

17. A
PV = -$950
n = 5
FV = $1,300
PMT = 0
i = ? = 6.5

18. B

$$NPV = CF_0 + \frac{CF_1}{(1 + r)^1} + \frac{CF_2}{(1 + r)^2} + \frac{CF_3}{(1 + r)^3} + \frac{CF_4}{(1 + r)^4} + \frac{CF_5}{(1 + r)^5}$$

$$NPV = -\$32,000 + \frac{\$19,000}{(1.06)^1} + \frac{\$6,000}{(1.06)^2} + \frac{\$12,000}{(1.06)^3} + \frac{\$14,000}{(1.06)^4} + \frac{\$3,000}{(1.06)^5}$$

NPV = -$32,000 + $17,924.53 + $5,339.98 + $10,075.43 + $11,089.31 + $2,241.77

NPV = $14,671.02

19. B
PMT = –$3,000
n = 7 × 2 = 14
i = 5 / 2 = 2.5
FV = 0
PV = ? = $35,072.74

20. B
Step 1: NPV = Present value of inflows – Present value of outflows
    NPV = $950,000 – $900,000 = $50,000
Step 2: Value of company prior to investment = $14.00 per share × 80,000 shares =
    $1,120,000
Step 3: Value of company after investment = $1,120,000 + $50,000 = $1,170,000

21. A
Step 1: NPV = Present value of inflows – Present value of outflows
    NPV = $950,000 – $900,000 = $50,000
Step 2: Increase in price per share = $50,000 / 80,000 shares = $0.63
Step 3: New share price = $14.00 + $0.63 = $14.63

22. D
FV = $1,000
n = 4 × 2 = 8
i = 7.98 / 2 = 3.99
PMT = 0
PV = ? = $731.25

23. A
PV = –$920
n = 4 × 2 = 8
PMT = $1,000 × 0.12 = $120, then $120 / 2 = $60
FV = $1,000
i = ? = 7.3584 × 2 = 14.72

24. C
FV = $1,000
n = 7 × 2 = 14
i = 11.2 / 2 = 5.6
PMT = $1000 × 0.09 = $90, then $90 / 2 = $45
PV = ? = $895.17

25. D
PV = –$4,000
n = 5 × 52 = 260
FV = $9,000
PMT = 0
i = ? = 0.3124 × 52 = 16.24

26. C
PV = −$965
n = 3 × 2 = 6
PMT = $1,000 × 0.07 = $70, then $70 / 2 = $35
FV = $1,000
i = ? = 4.1714 × 2 = 8.34

27. B
PV = −$840
n = 3 × 2 = 6
FV = $1,000
PMT = 0
i = ? = 2.949 × 2 = 5.90

28. A
FV = $1,000
i = 8.8 / 2 = 4.4
n = 5 × 2 = 10
PMT = $1,000 × 0.06 = $60, then $60 / 2 = $30
PV = ? = $888.68

29. A
Step 1: Net income = $50,000 − $15,000 = $35,000
Step 2: Maximum annual consumer debt = $35,000 × 0.2 = $7,000
Step 3: Maximum monthly consumer debt = $7,000 / 12 months = $583.33
Consumer debt payments, such as credit cards and auto loans, should not exceed 20% of net income.

30. C
Step 1: Maximum annual housing debt = $100,000 × 0.28 = $28,000
Step 2: Maximum monthly housing debt = $28,000 / 12 months = $2,333.33
Housing debt costs, including principal, interest, taxes, and insurance, should not exceed 28% of gross income.

31. C
Step 1: Maximum annual total debt = $80,000 × 0.36 = $28,800
Step 2: Maximum monthly total debt = $28,800 / 12 months = $2,400
Total debt payment should not exceed 36% of gross income.

32. A
Step 1: Maximum annual PITI = $75,000 × 0.28 = $21,000
Step 2: Maximum monthly PITI = $21,000 / 12 months = $1,750

33. D
Step 1: Maximum mortgage = $95,000 × 2.5 = $237,500
Step 2: Maximum purchase price = $237,500 / (1 − 0.2) = $296,875

34. B
Step 1: Monthly interest rate = 0.0475 / 12 months = 0.0039583
Step 2: Loan balance = $610 / 0.0039583 = $154,106.56

35. B
Step 1: Annual interest = $300,000 × 0.04 = $12,000
Step 2: Monthly interest = $12,000 / 12 months = $1,000
Step 3: Principal reduction from first payment = $1,500 – $1,000 = $500
Step 4: New loan balance = $300,000 – $500 = $299,500
Step 5: New annual interest = $299,500 × 0.04 = $11,980
Step 6: New monthly interest = $11,980 / 12 months = $998
Step 7: Principal reduction from second payment: $1,500 – $998 = $502

36. C
Step 1: Annual interest payment = $4,600 × 4 quarters = $18,400
Step 2: Annual interest rate = $18,400 / $230,000 = 0.08 = 8%

37. A
Step 1: Nicole's equity before trade = $185,000
Step 2: Justin's equity before trade = $350,000 – $40,000 = $310,000
Step 3: Difference in equity = $310,000 – $185,000 = $125,000; A fair trade requires Nicole to pay Justin $125,000.

38. A
Step 1: Monthly interest rate = 0.0425 / 12 months = 0.0035417
Step 2: Loan balance = $1,243.66 / 0.0035417 = $351,147.75

39. B
Step 1: Number of payments = 20 years × 12 months = 240
Step 2: Total amount of payments = 240 × $1,584.96 = $380,390.40
Step 3: Total interest paid = $380,390.40 – $247,350.00 = $133,040.40

40. D
Step 1: Monthly interest rate = 0.06 / 12 months = 0.005
Step 2: Monthly interest = $300,000 × 0.005 = $1,500
Step 3: Total interest paid = $1,500 × 3 months = $4,500

41. B
Step 1: Annual interest = $250,000 × 0.048 = $12,000
Step 2: Monthly interest = $12,000 / 12 months = $1,000
Step 3: Principal reduction from first payment = $1,951.04 – $1,000.00 = $951.04
Step 4: New loan balance = $250,000 – $951.04 = $249,048.96

42. B
Step 1: Monthly interest rate = 0.06 / 12 months = 0.005
Step 2: Monthly interest = $140,000 × 0.005 = $700

43. A
Step 1: Monthly interest rate = 0.06 / 12 months = 0.005
Step 2: Monthly interest = $140,000 × 0.005 = $700
Step 3: Principal reduction from first payment = $1,003 – $700 = $303

44. C
Step 1: Annual interest = $60,000 × 0.0525 = $3,150
Step 2: Monthly interest = $3,150 / 12 months = $262.50

45. D
Loan-to-value = $613,564 / $902,300 = 0.68 = 68%

46. D
Annual interest = $592,300 × 0.04625 = $27,393.88

47. B
Step 1: Number of payments = 30 years × 12 months = 360
Step 2: Total amount of payments = 360 × $1,930.48 = $694,972.80
Step 3: Total interest paid = $694,972.80 – $340,000.00 = $354,972.80

48. B
Step 1: Monthly interest rate = 0.075 / 12 months = 0.00625
Step 2: Mortgage balance = $612.50 / 0.00625 = $98,000

49. B
First year interest payment = $120,000 × 0.05 = $6,000

50. C
Step 1: First year interest payment = $120,000 × 0.05 = $6,000
Step 2: First month interest payment = $6,000 / 12 months = $500

51. B
Step 1: First year interest payment = $120,000 × 0.05 = $6,000
Step 2: First month interest payment = $6,000 / 12 months = $500
Step 3: First month principal payment = $700 – $500 = $200

52. B
Step 1: First year interest payment = $120,000 × 0.05 = $6,000
Step 2: First month interest payment = $6,000 / 12 months = $500
Step 3: First month principal payment = $700 – $500 = $200
Step 4: Loan balance after first payment = $120,000 – $200 = $119,800

53. D
Step 1: Annual interest = $5,600 × 2 periods = $11,200
Step 2: Annual interest rate = $11,200 / $224,000 = 0.05 = 5%

54. A
Owner's equity = $320,000 – $240,000 = $80,000

55. C
Step 1: Owner's equity = $320,000 – $240,000 = $80,000
Step 2: Debt-to-equity = $240,000 / $80,000 = 3:1

56. B

$85,000 – $67,000 = $18,000.

Accounts receivable (an asset) increases by $85,000. The balance in inventory (an asset) decreases by $67,000. The net increase in assets is $18,000.

57. C

Assets = Liabilities at year-end + Contributed capital at year-end + Beginning retained earnings + Revenues – Expenses – Dividends

Assets = $985 + $440 + $510 + $6,115 – $3,770 = $4,280 million

58. A

Debt-to-capital ratio = Total debt / (Total debt + Shareholders' equity)

Debt-to-capital ratio = $615,000 / ($615,000 + $205,000 + $230,000) = 0.59

59. C

$65,000 + $6,500 + $2,300 + $1,900 = $75,700

Repainting the factory is not included because it is not necessary for the machine to be ready to use.

60. A

Assets = Liabilities at year-end + Contributed capital at year-end + Beginning retained earnings + Revenues – Expenses – Dividends

Total assets = $500,000 + $100,000 + $150,000 + 300,000 – $200,000 – $50,000

Total assets = $800,000

61. C

Ending retained earnings = Beg. retained earnings + Net income – Distributions to owners

Ending retained earnings = $625 + $350 – $195 = $780 million

62. C

Owners' equity = Contributed capital + Retained earnings

Owners' equity = $1.3 million + $2.8 million = $4.1 million

63. C

Book value = Total assets – Total liabilities

Book value = $3,250,000 – $2,980,000 = $270,000

64. A

Debt-to-capital ratio = Total debt / (Total debt + Shareholders' equity)

Debt-to-capital = $44,100 / ($44,100 + $57,500) = 0.434 = 43.4%

65. B

Step 1: Net operating income = $36,000 – $12,000 = $24,000

Step 2: Property value = $24,000 / 0.14 = $171,428.57

66. A

Step 1: Annual potential gross income = $55,000 × 12 months = $660,000

Step 2: Vacancy allowance = $660,000 × 0.07 = $46,200

Step 3: Net operating income = $660,000 – $46,200 = $613,800

Step 4: Property value = $613,800 / 0.1 = $6,138,000

67. A
Step 1: Mortgage amount = $695,000 × (1 – 0.15) = $590,750
Step 2: Amount seller will owe for points = $590,750 × 0.015 = $8,861.25

68. D
Step 1: Mortgage amount = $220,000 × 0.85 = $187,000
Step 2: Closing costs = $187,000 × 0.0175 = $3,272.50

69. A
2 quarters – 1 quarter = 1 quarter
An economic recession is defined as a decline in real GDP for 2 or more consecutive quarters.

70. C
6 quarters – 3 quarters = 3 quarters
An economic depression is defined as a decline in real GDP for 6 or more consecutive quarters.

71. B
Gross Domestic Product (GDP) = C + I + G + E
C = Personal consumption
I = Gross private domestic investment
G = Government spending
E = Net exports

72. C
GDP = C + I + G + (X – M)
GDP = $11.4 + $6.2 + $3.3 + ($1.8 – $2.9) = $19.8 billion

73. B
GDP includes the value of final goods only. In this example, the value of the final goods is the retail price of $12.00.

74. C
($50 per card × 4 cards) + $30 = $230
David's loss is limited to $50 per credit card. However, one card has only $30 charged against it, so his loss is limited to $30 for that card.

75. C
5 × $15,000 = $75,000
A donor may contribute a total of five gift tax annual exclusion amounts on a one-time basis every five years to a 529 plan.

SECTION 2

LIFE AND DISABILITY INSURANCE

QUESTIONS

1. John is married and has a 10-year-old daughter. He earns an annual salary of $95,000, and if he dies his wife will receive $14,000 per year from Social Security. How much life insurance does John need in order to provide an equivalent income, without invading principal, if the money can earn a 6.5% return?

   A. $1,203,265
   B. $1,279,372
   C. $1,327,154
   D. $1,385,391

2. If Ashley dies, she wants to provide her husband with an annual income of $60,000 that will increase with inflation. If the money can earn an 8% return, and inflation is expected to average 3%, how much life insurance does Ashley need?

   A. $917,143
   B. $1,183,156
   C. $1,260,000
   D. $2,060,000

3. Tim, age 63, is provided with a $125,000 group term life insurance policy from his employer. He contributes $0.10 per $1,000 of coverage per month. What amount is included in Tim's income if the monthly rate is $0.66 per $1,000 of coverage?

   A. $438
   B. $440
   C. $442
   D. $444

The following information relates to questions 4 – 6.
Melissa owns a life insurance policy on her life with a cash value of $117,000. She has paid a total of $78,000 in premiums and has received $26,000 in dividends.

4. What is Melissa's basis in the policy?

   A. $0
   B. $52,000
   C. $78,000
   D. $91,000

5. If Melissa were to surrender the policy, what would be her realized gain?

   A. $0
   B. $26,000
   C. $52,000
   D. $65,000

6. If Melissa exchanged her policy in a Section 1035 exchange, how much tax would be payable in the current year?

A. $0
B. $26,000
C. $42,000
D. $75,000

7. Alpha Corporation is owned equally by Robert and Michelle. They are considering a cross-purchase agreement. If the business is worth $1,600,000, how should the life insurance policy on Robert be written?

A. $800,000 face amount with Michelle as owner and Robert as beneficiary.
B. $800,000 face amount with Michelle as owner and beneficiary.
C. $800,000 face amount with Robert as owner and Michelle as beneficiary.
D. $1,600,000 face amount with Robert as owner and beneficiary.

8. If a $500,000 life insurance policy has a cost of $0.35 per $100, the premium is:

A. $1,750.
B. $2,000.
C. $2,250.
D. $2,500.

9. If a $2,250,000 life insurance policy has a cost of $1.80 per $1,000, the premium is:

A. $3,150.
B. $3,600.
C. $3,750.
D. $4,050.

10. Richard purchased a $250,000 life insurance policy on his own life and gave it to his son, Nathan, who later sold it to Nathan's daughter, Rachel. When Nathan dies, what are the tax consequences?

A. Richard's estate must pay ordinary income tax on $250,000.
B. Nathan must pay ordinary income tax on $250,000, less the amount he sold the policy for.
C. Rachel must pay ordinary income tax on $250,000, less the amount she paid for the policy and any premiums she paid after the transfer occurred.
D. The death proceeds are paid to Rachel and no tax is due.

11. If Paul's employment was terminated 7 days ago, then he has _____ remaining to convert his group term life insurance policy to an individual life insurance policy.

A. 24 days
B. 31 days
C. 60 days
D. 83 days

12. Joe entered into a life buy-sell agreement with his business partner, Karen. Joe's basis in the business is $375,000 and the buyout is for $850,000. How much income will be taxable to Joe's family if he dies?

   A. $0
   B. $200,000
   C. $800,000
   D. $1,000,000

13. Kathy, age 60, is listed as beneficiary of her brother's $350,000 life insurance policy. Kathy is single and pays 20% federal taxes and 10% state taxes. If her brother were to die, how much tax would Kathy owe?

   A. $0
   B. $35,000
   C. $70,000
   D. $105,000

The following information relates to questions 14 – 15.
Jeff was recently diagnosed with a rare disease and is expected to live 5 more years. His life insurance policy has a face value of $500,000, and he could sell the policy to a viatical company for $280,000. Jeff has paid premiums of $3,200 per year for the last 9 years, and the cash value is currently $31,000.

14. If Jeff were to sell his policy to the viatical company today, his taxable gain would be:

   A. $0.
   B. $220,200.
   C. $251,200.
   D. $280,000.

15. If Jeff's life expectancy was 20 months and he sold his policy to the viatical company today, his taxable gain would be:

   A. $0.
   B. $220,200.
   C. $251,200.
   D. $280,000.

16. Lauren is an employee of Beta Corporation. As an employee, Lauren does not have to report any income with respect to the first _____ of life insurance coverage provided by Beta Corporation through a group plan.

   A. $25,000
   B. $50,000
   C. $75,000
   D. $100,000

The following information relates to questions 17 – 18.
Chris, age 51, is an employee of Sigma Corporation and earns an annual salary of $90,000. He receives 4 times his annual salary in group term life insurance. Non-key employees are only eligible for coverage equal to 1 times their annual salary.

17. If the monthly rate is $0.23 per $1,000, what amount will be included in Chris's income?

    A. $0
    B. $441.60
    C. $717.60
    D. $993.60

18. If Chris were eligible to receive coverage equal to 1 times his annual salary as a non-key employee, what amount would be included in his income?

    A. $0
    B. $110.40
    C. $179.40
    D. $248.40

The following information relates to questions 19 – 22.
Mel owns a life insurance contract with a basis of $220,000 and a cash value of $308,000. Earlier this year she borrowed $110,000 from the policy's cash value. Assume the policy is a modified endowment contract (MEC).

19. What portion of the loan is taxable?

    A. $0
    B. $88,000
    C. $110,000
    D. $198,000

20. If Mel is in the 28% tax bracket, how much tax must she pay on the loan?

    A. $0
    B. $24,640
    C. $30,800
    D. $55,440

21. What penalty must Mel pay that is attributed to the loan?

    A. $0
    B. $4,400
    C. $8,800
    D. $17,600

22. What is Mel's new basis in the policy after taking the loan?

    A. $88,000
    B. $198,000
    C. $220,000
    D. $308,000

The following information relates to questions 23 – 24.

Eric, age 44, is Vice President of Zeta Corporation. He receives $280,000 of group term life insurance coverage from his employer, which is equal to two times his annual salary. Assume the monthly rate is $0.10 per $1,000.

23. What is Eric's taxable economic benefit?

    A. $0
    B. $60
    C. $276
    D. $336

24. If Eric paid $120 toward the annual premium, what would be his new taxable economic benefit?

    A. $124
    B. $156
    C. $188
    D. $336

25. Megan, age 45, purchased a single-premium whole life insurance policy several years ago with a face value of $300,000. Her premium payment was $85,000, and the cash value has accumulated to $175,000. Assume the policy is a modified endowment contract (MEC), and Megan is in the 20% tax bracket. Including any applicable taxes and penalties, what is the total amount that Megan will owe if she borrows $25,000 from the policy this year?

    A. $0
    B. $9,000
    C. $18,000
    D. $27,000

26. If the annual net level premium for a $50,000 seven-pay policy is $1,300, then any similar policy for the same insured on which aggregate premiums exceed _____ during the first three policy years will be deemed a modified endowment contract (MEC).

    A. $1,300
    B. $2,600
    C. $3,900
    D. $5,200

27. If the annual net level premium for a $750,000 seven-pay policy is $6,200, then any similar policy for the same insured on which aggregate premiums exceed _____ during the first seven policy years will be deemed a modified endowment contract (MEC).

   A. $6,200
   B. $31,000
   C. $37,200
   D. $43,400

The following information relates to questions 28 – 29.
For the past 8 years, Jacob has paid $9,000 per year into a whole life insurance policy. Today his basis is $72,000 and the cash value is $58,000.

28. If Jacob exchanges his current whole life policy for a new policy, what will his new basis be?

   A. $0
   B. $58,000
   C. $72,000
   D. $130,000

29. If Jacob surrenders his current whole life policy and uses the cash value to purchase a new policy, what will his new basis be?

   A. $0
   B. $58,000
   C. $72,000
   D. $130,000

30. If Gamma Corporation has four owners, how many life insurance policies will be purchased if a cross-purchase agreement is used?

   A. 4 policies
   B. 8 policies
   C. 12 policies
   D. 16 policies

31. Emily purchases a $50,000 policy on the life of her husband, William, and names their daughter, Joan, as beneficiary. If William dies in 2018, Emily will be deemed to have made a gift to Joan in the amount of:

   A. $0.
   B. $15,000.
   C. $30,000.
   D. $50,000.

The following information relates to questions 32 – 33.
Sue owns a term life insurance policy with a $250,000 death benefit. She purchased the policy 6 years ago and has paid $1,600 per year in premiums. Sue also owns a whole life insurance policy with a $200,000 death benefit and a $95,000 cash surrender value. She purchased the whole life insurance policy 9 years ago and has paid $1,900 per year in premiums. Assume that Sue is in the 25% tax bracket.

32. If Sue's whole life policy paid her $9,000 in dividends, how much will she owe in taxes?

    A. $0
    B. $2,275
    C. $2,500
    D. $2,750

33. If Sue were to terminate the term life insurance policy, her taxable gain would be:

    A. $0.
    B. $62,500.
    C. $187,500.
    D. $250,000.

34. Albert sold his $70,000 life insurance policy to a viatical company for $52,500. The company paid an $86 monthly premium for 3 years before Albert died. What are the tax consequences to the viatical company in the year of Albert's death?

    A. $3,096 capital gains
    B. $3,096 ordinary income
    C. $14,404 capital gains
    D. $14,404 ordinary income

35. David designated his son, Justin, as beneficiary of his life insurance policy. This year David died and Justin elected to receive the $50,000 death benefit using the fixed-period option over a 10-year period. If Justin is in the 25% tax bracket, what part of each $5,000 annual payment will be taxable to him?

    A. $0
    B. $1,250
    C. $3,750
    D. $5,000

36. A viatical company purchased Janet's $750,000 life insurance policy for $490,000. It paid additional premiums of $23,000 before Janet died. What are the tax consequences to the viatical company in the year of Janet's death?

    A. $237,000 capital gains
    B. $237,000 ordinary income
    C. $283,000 capital gains
    D. $283,000 ordinary income

The following information relates to questions 37 – 38.
Dan purchased a $200,000 universal life insurance policy several years and named his wife, Cindy, as beneficiary. Since the policy's inception, the cash value has grown to $65,000.

37. If Dan elected the increased death benefit option (Option B), how much will Cindy receive when Dan dies?

A. $135,000
B. $200,000
C. $265,000
D. $330,000

38. If Dan elected the level death benefit option (Option A), how much will Cindy receive when Dan dies?

A. $135,000
B. $200,000
C. $265,000
D. $330,000

The following information relates to questions 39 – 40.
Charlotte, age 44, was diagnosed with a terminal autoimmune disease and given a maximum life expectancy of eighteen months. Upon receiving the diagnosis, she immediately sold her $300,000 whole life insurance policy to a viatical company for $175,000. The cash value of Charlotte's policy at the time of the sale was $55,000. After the sale, the viatical company made five additional premium payments of $2,500 each before Charlotte died.

39. If Charlotte was in the 20% tax bracket, how much tax was she required to pay upon selling her policy to the viatical company?

A. $0
B. $11,000
C. $24,000
D. $35,000

40. When Charlotte died, what portion of the death benefit was taxable to the viatical company?

A. $0
B. $112,500
C. $187,500
D. $300,000

The following information relates to questions 41 – 42.
Bruce purchased a whole life insurance policy several years ago. He has provided the following information related to the policy.

Face amount	$250,000
Cash value	$87,500
Paid-up additions	$75,000
Cash value of paid-up additions	$50,000
Annual premium	$4,300
Annual dividend	$1,900

41. What is the current surrender value of Bruce's policy?

    A. $112,500
    B. $137,500
    C. $162,500
    D. $164,400

42. If Bruce dies, a death benefit of _____ will be paid to his beneficiary.

    A. $250,000
    B. $262,500
    C. $300,000
    D. $325,000

The following information relates to questions 43 – 44.
Christian purchased a whole life insurance policy several years ago. He has provided the following information related to the policy.

Guaranteed cash value	$90,000
Premiums billed	$80,000
Existing loan	$25,000
Dividends reducing premium	$5,000

43. What is the current surrender value of Christian's policy?

    A. $60,000
    B. $65,000
    C. $70,000
    D. $90,000

44. If Christian surrenders the policy, how much of the proceeds would be taxable?

    A. $15,000
    B. $25,000
    C. $55,000
    D. $65,000

45. Rita is terminally ill and has a life expectancy of one year. She has a whole life insurance policy with a death benefit of $1,000,000. The cash value of the policy is $100,000, and she has paid $50,000 in premiums over the life of the policy. If Rita sells the policy for $600,000 to a viatical company, what are the tax consequences to Rita?

    A. $450,000 will be tax-free, and $150,000 will be taxable.
    B. $500,000 will be tax-free, and $100,000 will be taxable.
    C. $550,000 will be tax-free, and $50,000 will be taxable.
    D. $600,000 will be tax-free.

The following information relates to questions 46 – 47.
Earlier this year, Alexander exchanged a $500,000 ordinary life insurance policy for an annuity. He paid $90,000 in premiums over the life of the policy, and the cash value at the time of the exchange was $62,000.

46. What is Alexander's basis in the annuity?

    A. $28,000
    B. $62,000
    C. $90,000
    D. $152,000

47. What would be Alexander's basis if he used $25,000 of dividends to reduce the premium?

    A. $62,000
    B. $65,000
    C. $90,000
    D. $115,000

The following information relates to questions 48 – 50.
Andrea and George each own 50% of Sigma Corporation. The company is valued at $900,000 and they are interested in creating a buy-sell agreement.

48. If they create a cross-purchase agreement, how should George's life insurance policy be structured?

    A. George should be the owner and beneficiary of a $450,000 policy on Andrea's life.
    B. George should be the owner and Andrea should be the beneficiary of a $450,000 policy on Andrea's life.
    C. Andrea should be the owner and beneficiary of a $450,000 policy on Andrea's life.
    D. Andrea should be the owner and George should be the beneficiary of a $450,000 policy on Andrea's life.

49. **If they create an entity purchase agreement, how should Andrea's life insurance policy be structured?**

   A. Sigma Corporation should be the owner and beneficiary of a $900,000 policy on Andrea's life.
   B. Sigma Corporation should be the owner and George should be the beneficiary of a $900,000 policy on Andrea's life.
   C. Sigma Corporation should be the owner and beneficiary of a $450,000 policy on Andrea's life.
   D. Sigma Corporation should be the owner and George should be the beneficiary of a $450,000 policy on Andrea's life.

50. **If Andrea's basis is $100,000 and she becomes disabled, Sigma Corporation will redeem stock for $450,000 and she will realize capital gains of:**

   A. $0.
   B. $100,000.
   C. $350,000.
   D. $450,000.

The following information relates to questions 51 – 52.
Pete owns a whole life insurance policy that includes a waiver-of-premium rider. The monthly premium is $400 and the death benefit is $750,000. Pete is in the 25% tax bracket.

51. **If Pete were to become disabled, the insurer would pay _____ of the premium.**

   A. 0%
   B. 25%
   C. 50%
   D. 100%

52. **If Pete were to die, the death benefit would be taxed at a rate of:**

   A. 0%.
   B. 25%.
   C. 75%.
   D. 100%.

53. **Anna entered into a disability buy-sell agreement with her business partner, Henry. Anna's basis in the business is $70,000 and the buyout is for $600,000. How much of the proceeds would be taxable to Anna if she becomes disabled?**

   A. $0
   B. $70,000
   C. $530,000
   D. $600,000

54. Rebecca purchased a disability policy with a base benefit of $3,500 per month and a Social Security rider that provides replacement of her projected $1,800 Social Security disability benefit. If she becomes disabled and receives $600 per month in Social Security benefits, the total monthly benefit paid by the insurance company will be:

   A. $3,500.
   B. $4,100.
   C. $4,700.
   D. $5,300.

The following information relates to questions 55 – 56.
Tom's disability policy will pay $6,000 per month for total disability. His normal earnings are $9,000 per month, and he is now back to work after a period of total disability. However, he is only able to work part-time and earn $6,000 per month.

55. If Tom's disability policy included a partial disability benefit, how much would he collect each month?

   A. $0
   B. $1,500
   C. $3,000
   D. $6,000

56. If Tom's disability policy included a residual disability benefit, how much would he receive per month?

   A. $0
   B. $2,000
   C. $2,500
   D. $3,000

57. Denise's employer provides her with disability coverage that will pay her 60% of her salary if she's disabled. The company adds the cost of the coverage to her W-2. If Denise's salary is $126,000 and she is in the 28% tax bracket, then she will receive a monthly after-tax disability benefit of _____ if she becomes disabled.

   A. $0
   B. $1,764
   C. $4,536
   D. $6,300

58. Anthony's employer offers contributory group disability coverage to its employees. If he contributes 50% of the premium, and his disability benefit is $5,400 per month, what will be the tax consequences to Anthony if he were to become disabled?

   A. $0 will be taxable, and $5,400 will be tax-free each month.
   B. $1,350 will be taxable, and $4,050 will be tax-free each month.
   C. $2,700 will be taxable, and $2,700 will be tax-free each month.
   D. $5,400 will be taxable, and $0 will be tax-free each month.

59. Katie is a self-employed architect with an annual income of $90,000. If she applies for an individual disability policy, her maximum monthly benefit will likely be between:

   A. $1,875 and $2,250.
   B. $3,750 and $4,875.
   C. $5,250 and $6,225.
   D. $6,000 and $6,750.

The following information relates to questions 60 – 62.
Charles, age 50, purchased a disability policy with a monthly base benefit of $4,200 and a Social Insurance Supplement (SIS) benefit of $800.

60. If Charles becomes disabled, how much would he receive from his policy each month if his monthly Social Security disability benefit is $500?

   A. $4,200
   B. $4,500
   C. $4,700
   D. $5,000

61. If Charles becomes disabled, but Social Security denies his claim for disability benefits, how much would he receive from his policy each month?

   A. $3,400
   B. $4,200
   C. $5,000
   D. $5,800

62. If Charles becomes disabled, and Social Security pays him a monthly benefit of $1,100, how much would he receive from his policy each month?

   A. $3,900
   B. $4,200
   C. $4,500
   D. $5,300

The following information relates to questions 63 – 64.
Barbara is a Vice President for Theta Corporation. She receives a salary continuation disability policy from her employer, and the company pays the entire premium each month. Barbara's benefit is $15,000 per month and she is in the 35% tax bracket.

63. If Barbara becomes disabled, what would be her after-tax monthly benefit?

   A. $5,250
   B. $7,500
   C. $9,750
   D. $15,000

64. If Barbara becomes disabled, but she had paid the premiums each month with after-tax dollars, what would be her after-tax monthly benefit?

    A. $5,250
    B. $7,500
    C. $9,750
    D. $15,000

65. Which of the following is the correct formula used to calculate the amount of each annual fixed annuity payment that can be excluded from an annuitant's ordinary income?

    A. Exclusion ratio = Investment in contract / Expected return
    B. Exclusion ratio = Expected return / Investment in contract
    C. Exclusion ratio = 1 – (Investment in contract / Expected return)
    D. Exclusion ratio = 1 – (Expected return / Investment in contract)

The following information relates to questions 66 – 67.
Mark, age 70, purchased a fixed annuity for $15,380. His expected return through the payout phase is $28,510.

66. The exclusion ratio for Mark's annuity is:

    A. 0%.
    B. 46.1%.
    C. 53.9%.
    D. 100%.

67. If Mark receives a monthly payment of $210.20, the portion that will be taxed as ordinary income is:

    A. $0.
    B. $96.90.
    C. $113.30.
    D. $210.20.

68. Which of the following is the correct formula used to calculate the amount of each annual variable annuity payment that can be excluded from an annuitant's ordinary income?

    A. Excluded amount = Number of years of expected return / Investment in contract
    B. Excluded amount = Investment in contract / Number of years of expected return
    C. Excluded amount = 1 – (Number of years of return / Investment in contract)
    D. Excluded amount = 1 – (Investment in contract / Number of years of return)

69. Carol, age 68, purchased a variable annuity for $26,880. The annuity provides annual variable payments for life. If Carol's life expectancy is 15 years, the amount of each $3,000 annual payment that can be excluded from ordinary income is:

A. $0.
B. $1,208.
C. $1,792.
D. $3,000.

The following information relates to questions 70 – 71.
Michael, age 65, will begin receiving benefits from a fixed annuity that he purchased 10 years ago for $32,000. The annual payments will be $4,400, and Michael's life expectancy is 21 years.

70. The exclusion ratio for Michael's annuity is:

A. 13.8%.
B. 34.6%.
C. 65.4%.
D. 100%.

71. What will be the tax consequences of each payment that Michael receives?

A. $1,522.40 will be tax-free, and $2,877.60 will be taxable.
B. $2,877.60 will be tax-free, and $1,522.40 will be taxable.
C. $3,740.30 will be tax-free, and $660.70 will be taxable.
D. $4,400 will be tax-free.

72. Earlier this year, Delta Corporation purchased an annuity to fund a supplemental executive retirement plan for its key employees. The purchase price was $490,000, and the accumulated gain for the current year is $78,000. If Delta Corporation will not pay benefits until the key employees retire in 5 years, what amount of the gain is taxable this year?

A. $0
B. $15,600
C. $27,300
D. $78,000

73. Briana, age 67, pays $212,000 for a fixed annuity that will pay her $18,000 per year for the rest of her life. If her life expectancy is 16 years, how much of each annual payment that will be taxable?

A. $4,752
B. $6,284
C. $11,716
D. $13,248

The following information relates to questions 74 – 76.
Don, age 65, purchased an annuity 24 years ago for $400,000. This year he began receiving payments of $3,000 per month, which will continue for the rest of his life. Assume that Don's life expectancy is 17 years, and he is in the 28% tax bracket.

74. The exclusion ratio for Don's annuity is:

    A. 34.6%.
    B. 44.2%.
    C. 55.8%.
    D. 65.4%.

75. How much of each payment that Don receives will be tax-free?

    A. $840
    B. $1,038
    C. $1,962
    D. $2,160

76. When the excluded (tax-free) payments exceed $400,000, what are the tax consequences for all future payments that Don receives?

    A. 28% of each payment will be tax-free.
    B. 72% of each payment will be tax-free.
    C. 100% of each payment will be tax-free.
    D. 100% of each payment will be taxable.

77. Erin, age 66, is planning to retire this year. She will begin receiving payments from an annuity that she purchased several years ago for $110,000. If her life expectancy is 19 years and the monthly annuity payment is $850, how much of each payment will be tax-free?

    A. $348.10
    B. $367.20
    C. $482.80
    D. $501.90

The following information relates to questions 78 – 80.
Edward, age 67, purchased an annuity 9 years ago for $86,000. The annuity is now worth $174,000, and he is receiving $1,900 per month based on his 16-year life expectancy.

78. The exclusion ratio for Edward's policy is:

    A. 23.6%.
    B. 24.1%.
    C. 24.8%.
    D. 25.2%.

79. How much of each payment that Edward receives will be tax-free?

    A. $448.40
    B. $823.80
    C. $1,076.20
    D. $1,451.60

80. How much of each payment that Edward receives will be taxable?

    A. $448.40
    B. $823.80
    C. $1,076.20
    D. $1,451.60

ANSWER KEY

1. C
Step 1: ($95,000 – $14,000) / 0.065 = $1,246,154
Step 2: Add income for year 1 = $81,000 + $1,246,154 = $1,327,154

2. C
Step 1: $60,000 / (0.08 – 0.03) = $1,200,000
Step 2: Add income for year 1 = $60,000 + $1,200,000 = $1,260,000

3. D
Step 1: $125,000 – $50,000 exemption = $75,000
Step 2: Monthly cost = ($75,000 × $0.66) / $1,000 = $49.50
Step 3: Monthly contribution = ($125,000 × $0.10) / $1,000 = $12.50
Step 4: ($49.50 – $12.50) × 12 months = $444

4. B
Basis = $78,000 – $26,000 = $52,000

5. D
Step 1: Basis = $78,000 – $26,000 = $52,000
Step 2: Realized gain = $117,000 – $52,000 = $65,000

6. A
No tax would be payable in the current year if Melissa exchanges her policy in a Section 1035 exchange.

7. B
In a cross-purchase agreement, the owners purchase life insurance on each other for their fractional share of business ownership.

8. A
Premium = ($500,000 × $0.35) / $100 = $1,750

9. D
Premium = ($2,250,000 × $1.80) / $1,000 = $4,050

10. C
When Nathan dies, Rachel must pay ordinary income tax on $250,000, less the amount she paid for the policy and any premiums she paid after the transfer occurred.

11. A
31 days – 7 days = 24 days
A group term life insurance policy can be converted to an individual life insurance policy within 31 days of an employee terminating employment.

12. A
At Joe's death, his estate will receive a step-up in basis and no tax will be due on the life insurance proceeds.

13. A
Kathy would not owe any tax because the death benefit from a life insurance policy is not taxable income.

14. C
Step 1: Premiums paid = $3,200 per year × 9 years = $28,800
Step 2: Taxable gain = $280,000 – $28,800 = $251,200
Since Jeff is expected to live longer than 24 months, he will not qualify for the tax exclusion. The amount of proceeds subject to taxation is the difference between the sale price and the premiums paid.

15. A
If Jeff's life expectancy is less than 24 months, the sale proceeds would be tax-free.

16. B
An employee does not have to report any income with respect to the first $50,000 of life insurance coverage provided by an employer through a group plan.

17. D
Step 1: $90,000 × 4 = $360,000
Step 2: ($360,000 × $0.23) / $1,000 = $82.80
Step 3: $82.80 × 12 months = $993.60
In a discriminatory group term life insurance policy, key employees lose the $50,000 exemption.

18. B
Step 1: $90,000 – $50,000 exemption = $40,000
Step 2: ($40,000 × $0.23) / $1,000 = $9.20
Step 3: $9.20 × 12 months = $110.40

19. B
Taxable portion of loan = $308,000 – $220,000 = $88,000

20. B
Step 1: Taxable portion of loan = $308,000 – $220,000 = $88,000
Step 2: Tax owed = $88,000 × 0.28 = $24,640

21. C
Step 1: Taxable portion of loan = $308,000 – $220,000 = $88,000
Step 2: Penalty owed = $88,000 × 0.1 = $8,800

22. D
Step 1: Taxable portion of loan = $308,000 – $220,000 = $88,000
Step 2: New basis = $220,000 + $88,000 = $308,000

23. C
Step 1: $280,000 – $50,000 exemption = $230,000
Step 2: ($230,000 × $0.10) / $1,000 = $23
Step 3: $23 × 12 months = $276

24. B
Step 1: $280,000 – $50,000 exemption = $230,000
Step 2: ($230,000 × $0.10) / $1,000 = $23
Step 3: $23 × 12 months = $276
Step 4: $276 – $120 = $156

25. D
Step 1: Taxable portion of loan = $175,000 – $85,000 = $90,000
Step 2: Tax owed = $90,000 × 0.2 = $18,000
Step 3: Penalty owed = $90,000 × 0.1 = $9,000
Step 4: Total amount owed = $18,000 + $9,000 = $27,000

26. C
$1,300 per year × 3 years = $3,900
If the annual net level premium for a $50,000 seven-pay policy is $1,300, then any similar policy for the same insured on which aggregate premiums exceed $3,900 during the first three policy years will be deemed a modified endowment contract (MEC).

27. D
$6,200 per year × 7 years = $43,400
If the annual net level premium for a $750,000 seven-pay policy is $6,200, then any similar policy for the same insured on which aggregate premiums exceed $43,400 during the first seven policy years will be deemed a modified endowment contract (MEC).

28. C
Jacob's basis of $72,000 carries over to the new policy in a Section 1035 exchange.

29. B
Jacob's new policy would have a basis equal to the cash value of his current policy, which is $58,000.

30. C
4 owners × 3 policies per owner = 12 policies
If a company has 4 owners, then 12 life insurance policies will be purchased if a cross-purchase agreement is used.

31. D
If William dies in 2018, Emily will be deemed to have made a gift to Joan in the amount of $50,000.

32. A
Cash dividends from a life insurance policy are generally treated as a return of principal and are not taxable income.

33. A
Sue would have no taxable gain if she terminates her term life insurance policy.

34. D
Step 1: $70,000 – $52,500 = $17,500
Step 2: $86 per month × 12 months × 3 years = $3,096

Step 3: $17,500 – $3,096 = $14,404
The viatical company must report the gain as ordinary income.

35. A
The $5,000 annual payment is not taxable to Justin, but any amount received in excess of $5,000 will be taxable.

36. B
Gain = $750,000 – $490,000 – $23,000 = $237,000
The viatical company must report the gain as ordinary income.

37. C
Total payout to Cindy = $200,000 + $65,000 = $265,000
With Option B, Cindy will receive the death benefit plus the cash value.

38. B
With Option A, Cindy will receive the death benefit only.

39. A
Because Charlotte's life expectancy was less than 24 months, the sale proceeds were tax-free.

40. B
Step 1: Premium payments = $2,500 per year × 5 years = $12,500
Step 2: Viatical company's basis = $175,000 + $12,500 = $187,500
Step 3: Taxable amount = $300,000 – $187,500 = $112,500

41. B
Surrender value = $87,500 + $50,000 = $137,500

42. D
Death benefit = $250,000 + $75,000 = $325,000

43. B
Surrender value = $90,000 – $25,000 = $65,000

44. A
Taxable portion = $90,000 – ($80,000 – $5,000) = $15,000

45. D
Because Rita's life expectancy is less than 24 months, the sale proceeds will be tax-free.

46. C
Alexander's basis in the annuity is $90,000, which represents his premium payments in the life insurance policy.

47. B
$90,000 – $25,000 = $65,000
Alexander's basis would have been equal to the premium payments ($90,000) less the dividends used to reduce the premium ($25,000).

48. A

In a cross-purchase agreement, George should be the owner and beneficiary of a $450,000 policy on Andrea's life.

49. C

In an entity purchase agreement, Sigma Corporation should be the owner and beneficiary of a $450,000 policy on Andrea's life.

50. C

Realized capital gain = $450,000 – $100,000 = $350,000

51. D

Because Pete owns a whole life insurance policy that includes a waiver-of-premium rider, if he were to become disabled, the insurer would pay 100% of the premium.

52. A

Pete would not owe any tax because the death benefit from a life insurance policy is not taxable income.

53. C

Taxable amount = $600,000 – $70,000 = $530,000

54. C

Disability benefit = $3,500 + ($1,800 – $600) = $4,700

55. C

A partial disability benefit is typically 50% of the total disability benefit. Of the choices provided, $3,000 is the best estimate.

56. B

Step 1: Reduction in earnings = ($9,000 – $6,000) / $9,000 = 0.333̄3̄
Step 2: Amount Tom will receive = $6,000 × 0.333̄3̄ = $2,000

57. D

Step 1: Monthly salary = $126,000 / 12 months = $10,500
Step 2: Monthly disability benefit = $10,500 × 0.6 = $6,300
Because Denise's employer adds the premium cost to her W-2, she is paying for the coverage. Therefore, the benefits are not taxable.

58. C

$5,400 × 0.5 = $2,700
Because Anthony is paying 50% of the premium with after-tax dollars, 50% of the benefits will be tax-free, and the other 50% will be taxable.

59. B

Step 1: Monthly income = $90,000 / 12 months = $7,500
Step 2: Approximate minimum disability benefit = $7,500 × 0.5 = $3,750
Step 3: Approximate maximum disability benefit = $7,500 × 0.65 = $4,875
Katie's maximum monthly benefit will likely be between 50% and 65% of her income.

60. B
Disability benefit = $4,200 + ($800 – $500) = $4,500

61. C
Disability benefit = $4,200 + $800 = $5,000

62. B
Charles will receive his base disability benefit of $4,200.

63. C
After-tax monthly benefit = $15,000 × (1 – 0.35) = $9,750

64. D
If Barbara paid the premiums with after-tax dollars, the benefits would be tax-free.

65. A
Exclusion ratio = Investment in contract / Expected return

66. C
Exclusion ratio = $15,380 / $28,510 = 0.539 = 53.9%

67. B
Step 1: Exclusion ratio = $15,380 / $28,510 = 0.539
Step 2: Amount excluded from ordinary income = $210.20 × 0.539 = $113.30
Step 3: Amount included as ordinary income = $210.20 – $113.30 = $96.90

68. B
Exclusion ratio = Investment in contract / Number of years of expected return

69. C
Amount excluded from ordinary income = $26,880 / 15 years = $1,792

70. B
Step 1: Total payments expected = $4,400 per year × 21 years = $92,400
Step 2: Exclusion ratio = $32,000 / $92,400 = 0.346 = 34.6%

71. A
Step 1: Total payments expected = $4,400 per year × 21 years = $92,400
Step 2: Exclusion ratio = $32,000 / $92,400 = 0.346
Step 3: Tax-free portion = $4,400 × 0.346 = $1,522.40
Step 4: Taxable portion = $4,400 – $1,522.40 = $2,877.60

72. D
Because Delta Corporation is a non-natural person, it must report the accumulated gain in the annuity as ordinary income.

73. A
Step 1: Total payments expected = $18,000 per year × 16 years = $288,000
Step 2: Exclusion ratio = $212,000 / $288,000 = 0.736
Step 3: Taxable portion = $18,000 × (1 – 0.736) = $4,752

74. D
Step 1: Total payments expected = \$3,000 per month × 12 months × 17 years = \$612,000
Step 2: Exclusion ratio = \$400,000 / \$612,000 = 0.654 = 65.4%

75. C
Step 1: Total payments expected = \$3,000 per month × 12 months × 17 years = \$612,000
Step 2: Exclusion ratio = \$400,000 / \$612,000 = 0.654
Step 3: Tax-free portion = \$3,000 × 0.654 = \$1,962

76. D
When the excluded (tax-free) payments of \$1,962 total \$400,000 (204 payments), all future payments will be fully taxable to Don.

77. C
Step 1: Total payments expected = \$850 per month × 12 months × 19 years = \$193,800
Step 2: Exclusion ratio = \$110,000 / \$193,800 = 0.568
Step 3: Tax-free portion = \$850 × 0.568 = \$482.80

78. A
Step 1: Total payments expected = \$1,900 per month × 12 months × 16 years = \$364,800
Step 2: Exclusion ratio = \$86,000 / \$364,800 = 0.236 = 23.6%

79. A
Step 1: Total payments expected = \$1,900 per month × 12 months × 16 years = \$364,800
Step 2: Exclusion ratio = \$86,000 / \$364,800 = 0.236
Step 3: Tax-free portion = \$1,900 × 0.236 = \$448.40

80. D
Step 1: Total payments expected = \$1,900 per month × 12 months × 16 years = \$364,800
Step 2: Exclusion ratio = \$86,000 / \$364,800 = 0.236
Step 3: Taxable portion = \$1,900 × (1 – 0.236) = \$1,451.60

SECTION 3

INCOME PLANNING

QUESTIONS

1. Marcus, a self-employed taxpayer, did not incur any income tax liability for the preceding year, but failed to withhold $8,000 in tax payments in the current year. What penalty will Marcus be required to pay?

A. $0
B. $800
C. $1,600
D. $8,000

2. Kathy has self-employment income of $68,000 for the current year. How much self-employment tax must she pay?

A. $7,913
B. $8,034
C. $9,608
D. $10,172

3. Dan (AGI of $180,000) donated mutual funds to a local school with a fair market value of $100,000. He purchased the stock 8 months ago for $95,000. What is Dan's maximum allowable charitable deduction for the current year?

A. $85,000
B. $90,000
C. $95,000
D. $100,000

4. Olivia works as a self-employed graphic designer, and last year she had an AGI of $120,000 and she paid $33,000 in income taxes. She expects her tax liability to be $29,000 this year. What is the minimum estimated tax payment Olivia must make to avoid the underpayment penalty?

A. $0
B. $26,100
C. $29,000
D. $33,000

5. Alpha Inc., an S Corp, was started 6 years ago for $73,000 cash. Due to unforeseen legal troubles, the owner, William, had to lend the company another $40,000 to stay in operation. This year, Alpha Inc. has a net operating loss of $127,000. How much can William deduct as a loss on his tax return?

A. $73,000
B. $87,000
C. $113,000
D. $127,000

6. Sebastian, an individual taxpayer, donated $51,200 to a public charity last year when his gross income was $97,280. This year, when his gross income is $102,400, he makes no donations to charity. Sebastian could deduct _____ last year and _____ this year.

A. $25,600; $5,120
B. $28,800; $22,400
C. $48,640; $2,560
D. $51,200; $0

7. Emily (AGI of $132,000) has an investment interest expense of $11,000 from her margin account, and has $9,500 of investment income. She paid her investment advisor $6,200 for investment advice this year. How much investment interest expense can Emily deduct?

A. $3,560
B. $4,800
C. $5,940
D. $11,000

8. The Johnsons, a married couple filing a joint tax return, purchased a principal residence in 2015 for $320,000. If they sold the house in 2016 for $390,000, what portion of the gain is subject to capital gains tax?

A. $0
B. $70,000
C. $250,000
D. $500,000

9. Stephanie purchased a principal residence in 2013 for $700,000. If she sold the house in 2016 for $850,000, what portion of the gain is subject to capital gains tax?

A. $0
B. $25,000
C. $250,000
D. $500,000

10. Harold purchased a principal residence in 2012 for $175,000. If he sold the house in 2017 for $450,000, what portion of the gain is subject to capital gains tax?

A. $0
B. $25,000
C. $250,000
D. $500,000

11. The Millers, a married couple filing a joint tax return, purchased a principal residence in 2013 for $450,000. If they sold the house in 2017 for $575,000, what portion of the gain is subject to capital gains tax?

    A. $0
    B. $125,000
    C. $250,000
    D. $500,000

12. Luke pays $1,740 in property taxes for 6 months in advance on March 1st. If he sells his house on May 1st, how much will the buyer owe Luke?

    A. $435
    B. $580
    C. $1,160
    D. $1,305

13. The current value of Dawn's property, excluding the lot, is $255,000. If her property has depreciated 4.5% per year for the past 6 years, what was its original value?

    A. $186,150.00
    B. $266,675.00
    C. $290,322.58
    D. $349,315.07

14. Paul owns a 12-year-old property that is worth $339,500. If the property has depreciated at a rate of 2.5% per year, what was its original value?

    A. $480,000
    B. $485,000
    C. $490,000
    D. $495,000

15. If a property's economic life is 27.5 years, how much does it depreciate each year?

    A. 3.46%
    B. 3.64%
    C. 4.36%
    D. 4.63%

16. If an apartment building depreciates 2% per year, what is its economic life?

    A. 10 years
    B. 20 years
    C. 25 years
    D. 50 years

17. Mary purchased a property for $620,000. If it has a 20-year life, then it will be worth $372,000 in:

A. 7 years.
B. 8 years.
C. 9 years.
D. 10 years.

18. Nathan purchased a building for $410,000. If it has a total useful life of 25 years, then what will be its value after 7 years?

A. $293,600
B. $295,200
C. $302,700
D. $304,300

19. If an apartment building depreciates 3.5% per year, then it will be worth 30% of its original value in:

A. 9 years.
B. 12 years.
C. 17 years.
D. 20 years.

20. Joe purchased a building for $980,000. If it has a useful life of 25 years, then it will be worth $705,600 in:

A. 6 years.
B. 7 years.
C. 8 years.
D. 9 years.

The following information relates to questions 21 – 23.
Nora's income is $80,000 and she is in the 25% tax bracket. While preparing to file her tax return, she expected to take an $8,000 deduction that she qualified for. However, she has discovered the deduction has been replaced with a $4,000 tax credit.

21. Ignoring exemptions and other adjustments, if Nora had claimed the $8,000 tax deduction, her total taxes owed would have been:

A. $14,000.
B. $16,000.
C. $18,000.
D. $20,000.

22. Ignoring exemptions and other adjustments, if Nora claims the $4,000 tax credit, her total taxes owed will be:

  A. $14,000.
  B. $16,000.
  C. $18,000.
  D. $20,000.

23. Ignoring exemptions and other adjustments, a tax credit of _____ would result in the same amount of taxes owed as the $8,000 tax deduction.

  A. $2,000
  B. $3,000
  C. $5,000
  D. $6,000

24. Rob purchased an art sculpture for $9,500. Years later, when the sculpture was worth $4,500, he gave it to his brother, Bill, as a gift. A few months later, Bill sold the sculpture at auction for $3,500. Assuming Bill paid no gift taxes on the sculpture when he received it, what was his net gain or loss on the sale?

  A. $1,000 loss
  B. $3,500 gain
  C. $6,000 loss
  D. No gain or loss will be recognized.

25. Melissa, age 12, works after school in her mother's bakery. Her mother owns and operates the business as a sole proprietorship. Melissa is paid $8,000 per year for her work. What is Melissa's tax bracket for the majority of her earnings?

  A. Melissa's own tax bracket with a reduction for Social Security.
  B. Melissa's own tax bracket without a reduction for Social Security.
  C. Her mother's tax bracket with a reduction for Social Security.
  D. Her mother's tax bracket without a reduction for Social Security.

26. On September 12th of last year, Joel bought 100 shares of Sigma stock for $20 per share. On December 18th of last year, he sold all of his shares for $1,600. On January 3rd of this year, Joel bought back 100 shares of Sigma stock for $20 per share. Which of the following is true regarding Joel's transaction?

  A. Joel can realize the $400 loss.
  B. If Joel waited a few more days to buy back the stock, he could have realized the gain.
  C. The wash sale rule doesn't apply to Joel because the transactions occurred in two separate years.
  D. No loss deduction is allowed; the amount of the disallowed loss will be added to the cost basis of the shares that Joel purchased on January 3rd.

The following information relates to questions 27 – 29.
Jim had several capital gains and losses for the current year. His long-term capital gains were $3,200, his long-term capital losses were $2,800, his short-term capital gains were $800, and his short-term capital losses were $3,500.

27. What is the amount of net long-term capital gains?

    A. $0
    B. $400
    C. $700
    D. $2,400

28. What is the amount of net short-term capital gains?

    A. –$2,700
    B. –$700
    C. –$400
    D. $0

29. What is the total calculated capital gain or capital loss?

    A. $2,300 net short-term capital loss
    B. $2,300 net short-term capital gain
    C. $3,000 net short-term capital loss
    D. $3,000 net short-term capital gain

30. Last year, Constantine sold a parcel of vacant land to his local municipality for $225,000. The fair market value of the land at the time of the sale was $750,000. If Constantine's original basis in the land was $90,000, then what was the taxable gain resulting from the sale?

    A. $0
    B. $162,000
    C. $198,000
    D. $225,000

31. In 2016, Epsilon Corporation reported total expenses of $72,000 and net income of $90,000. If accounts receivable decreased by $12,000, then how much cash was received from customers?

    A. $102,000
    B. $150,000
    C. $162,000
    D. $174,000

32. Omega Corporation's taxable income is 19.3% of sales. Assuming their effective tax rate is 38%, and their dividend payout rate is 50%, what is the Omega Corporation's net profit margin?

    A. 10.12%
    B. 10.85%
    C. 11.97%
    D. 12.19%

33. In 2016, Delta Corporation sold an intangible asset and reported a loss of $400,000 on the sale. If the acquisition cost of the asset was $980,000, and accumulated depreciation was $300,000, what was the sale price?

    A. $100,000
    B. $280,000
    C. $580,000
    D. $1,080,000

The following information relates to questions 34 – 35.
In March 2016, Zeta Corp. purchased 6,200 units of product for a total cost of $118,000. In May 2016, the company purchased 3,800 additional units for a total cost of $74,000. Throughout the year, the company sold 7,500 units, generating revenue of $180,000.

34. According to the FIFO method, what was Zeta Corp.'s cost of goods sold for 2016?

    A. $138,712
    B. $143,297
    C. $155,385
    D. $163,820

35. According to the weighted average cost method, what was Zeta Corp.'s cost of goods sold for 2016?

    A. $144,000
    B. $146,000
    C. $148,000
    D. $150,000

The following information relates to questions 36 – 37.
In 2016, Kappa LLC reported tax expense of $780,000 and interest expense of $2.47 million. Taxes payable decreased by $520,000, and interest payable increased by $390,000.

36. What was the amount of interest paid?

    A. $1.56 million
    B. $2.08 million
    C. $2.47 million
    D. $2.86 million

37. What was the amount of taxes paid?

  A. $1.2 million
  B. $1.3 million
  C. $1.4 million
  D. $1.5 million

38. In 2016, Lambda Holding Company reported an annual cost of goods sold of $17.6 million. Total assets increased by $12.1 million, including an increase of $1.1 million in inventory. Total liabilities increased by $9.9 million, including an increase of $440,000 in accounts payable. Based on this information, how much cash was paid to suppliers?

  A. $10.34 million
  B. $16.94 million
  C. $18.26 million
  D. $18.70 million

39. Gamma Construction Company entered into a contract to build a medical facility. The building contract was for $900,000, and total construction costs were $550,000. If the company incurred costs of $225,000 in the first year, and those costs accurately reflected the progress towards completing the contract, then how much revenue must Gamma Construction Company recognize in the first year?

  A. $227,840
  B. $324,750
  C. $368,190
  D. $420,240

The following information relates to questions 40 – 41.
Theta Corporation provides the following information for the fiscal year (in millions):

Revenue	$51.5
Cost of goods sold	$29.0
Other operating expenses	$6.5
Interest expense	$1.1
Tax expense	$1.6
Effective tax rate	28%

40. What is Theta Corporation's gross profit?

  A. $6.5 million
  B. $13.3 million
  C. $22.5 million
  D. $23.6 million

41. What is Theta Corporation's net income?

A. $6.5 million
B. $13.3 million
C. $22.5 million
D. $23.6 million

42. Alpha Corporation reports the following information for the fiscal year:

Revenue	$2,875,000
Cost of goods sold	$1,950,000
Return of goods sold	$160,000
Cash collected	$1,425,000
Effective tax rate	30%

According to the accrual basis of accounting, what is Alpha Corporation's reported net revenue?

A. $925,000
B. $1,085,000
C. $1,585,000
D. $2,715,000

The following information relates to questions 43 – 44.
In January 2016, Beta Manufacturing Corporation purchased equipment for $490,000. The equipment has an estimated useful life of 8 years and an estimated residual value of $20,000.

43. According to the straight-line method, how much depreciation will Beta Manufacturing Corporation claim in 2017?

A. $58,750
B. $61,250
C. $63,750
D. $67,500

44. According to the double declining balance method, how much depreciation will Beta Manufacturing Corporation claim in 2016?

A. $30,625
B. $61,250
C. $122,500
D. $135,840

45. In January 2016, Sigma Construction Company entered into a contract to construct a building for a private medical practice. The construction will take 3 years to complete. The following information is provided at the end of 2016:

Total revenue agreed to by contract	$6,600,000
Total anticipated cost	$4,000,000
Costs incurred in 2016	$900,000

If Sigma Construction Company estimates percentage completed based on costs incurred as a percent of total estimated costs, then according to the completed contract method, how much revenue will the company report in 2016?

A. $0
B. $1,900,000
C. $2,200,000
D. $2,600,000

46. On January 1, 2016, Epsilon LLC sold land for $300,000. The original cost of the land was $180,000. The company received a down payment of $60,000, with the remaining balance to be paid in 2017. According to the installment method, how much profit will Epsilon LLC report in 2016?

A. $0
B. $24,000
C. $48,000
D. $72,000

47. In 2016, Omega LLC reported total revenue of $800,000, total expenses of $650,000, and net income of $150,000. If accounts receivable increased by $90,000, then how much cash did Omega LLC receive from customers?

A. $560,000
B. $710,000
C. $800,000
D. $890,000

48. Delta Manufacturing Company has provided the following information for a piece of equipment that it sold for $72,500 on December 31, 2016:

Acquisition cost of equipment	$95,000
Acquisition date	January 1, 2013
Estimated residual value at acquisition date	$11,250
Expected useful life	8 years
Depreciation method	Straight-line

What gain (or loss) must be reported on the sale of the equipment?

A. $25,275 loss
B. $19,375 gain
C. $25,375 gain
D. $30,350 gain

The following information relates to questions 49 – 50.

Zeta LLC reported the following inventory transactions for the year:

Date	Purchase	Sales
February 12, 2016	60 units at $42	18 units at $49
April 18, 2016	24 units at $56	49 units at $63
October 27, 2016	126 units at $70	84 units at $84

49. Assuming there was no inventory at the beginning of the year, the year-end inventory using the FIFO method is:

A. $3,684.
B. $3,996.
C. $4,130.
D. $4,934.

50. Assuming there was no inventory at the beginning of the year, the year-end inventory using the LIFO method is:

A. $2,478.
B. $2,660.
C. $3,042.
D. $4,482.

The following information relates to questions 51 – 53.

A research analyst provides the following information for Omikron Corporation's fiscal year:

Revenue	$550,000
Cost of sales	$325,000
Gross profit	$225,000
Marketing costs	$55,000
Operating income	$170,000
Interest and other expense, net	$20,000
Earnings before taxes	$150,000

51. What is Omikron Corporation's gross profit margin?

A. 27.3%
B. 40.9%
C. 59.1%
D. 63.7%

52. What is Omikron Corporation's operating profit margin?

A. 27.3%
B. 30.9%
C. 51.2%
D. 75.6%

53. What is Omikron Corporation's pretax margin?

   A. 27.3%
   B. 40.9%
   C. 53.5%
   D. 66.7%

54. Lambda Corporation provides the following information in its annual shareholder report:

Net income	$660,000
Depreciation	$35,000
Increase in accounts receivable	$110,000
Increase in accounts payable	$120,000

   What is Lambda Corporation's cash flow from operations?

   A. $685,000
   B. $705,000
   C. $890,000
   D. $925,000

55. In 2016, Kappa Manufacturing Corporation's beginning balance of salaries payable was $800,000. The company reported a total salary expense of $3.6 million and the ending balance of salaries payable was $500,000. How much cash did Kappa Manufacturing Corporation pay in salaries?

   A. $3.9 million
   B. $4.1 million
   C. $4.4 million
   D. $4.9 million

56. Gamma Corporation provides the following information about its investing activities for the fiscal year:

Cost to purchase new equipment	$90,000
Proceeds from selling old equipment	$80,000
Gain from selling old equipment	$30,000
Proceeds from issuing debt	$85,000

   Gamma Corporation's statement of cash flows would report net cash flow from investing activities equal to:

   A. –$10,000.
   B. $20,000.
   C. $50,000.
   D. $105,000.

The following information relates to questions 57 – 58.
In 2016, Theta Real Estate Company sold property for $1,800,000. They originally purchased the property in 2008 for $1,200,000. The company received $500,000 as a down payment from the buyer, with the remainder of the sales price to be received over a 7-year period.

57. **If the installment method is used, how much profit will be recognized attributable to the down payment?**

    A. $0
    B. $166,667
    C. $500,000
    D. $600,000

58. **If the cost recovery method is used, how much profit will be recognized attributable to the down payment?**

    A. $0
    B. $166,667
    C. $500,000
    D. $600,000

59. **The penalty for failing to pay taxes owed is _____ of the tax due, for each month or part of a month the tax remains unpaid, up to a maximum of _____.**

    A. 0.5%; 5%
    B. 0.5%; 25%
    C. 5%; 25%
    D. 5%; 50%

60. **The penalty for failing to file a tax return is _____ of the unpaid taxes, for each month or part of a month that the tax return is late, up to a maximum of _____.**

    A. 0.5%; 5%
    B. 0.5%; 25%
    C. 5%; 25%
    D. 5%; 50%

61. **Due to negligence, Spencer underpaid his taxes last year by $25,000. He will incur a penalty of :**

    A. $5,000.
    B. $6,250.
    C. $12,500.
    D. $18,750.

62. Due to civil fraud, Francesca underpaid her taxes last year by $10,000. She will incur a penalty of:

    A. $2,000.
    B. $2,500.
    C. $5,000.
    D. $7,500.

63. The penalty for a tax return preparer understating the amount of tax owed, not due to willful or reckless conduct, is the greater of _____ or _____ of the income derived by the tax return preparer with respect to the return or claim for refund.

    A. $500; 5%
    B. $1,000; 50%
    C. $2,000; 25%
    D. $5,000; 50%

64. Ben is faced with a tax deficiency of $8,260, which is the result of negligence. He's also faced with a tax deficiency of $4,000, which is the result of civil fraud. What is the amount of Ben's total penalty?

    A. $2,452
    B. $4,652
    C. $6,995
    D. $9,195

65. Cars, light-duty trucks, computers, and appliances have a _____ recovery period for depreciation purposes.

    A. 3-year
    B. 5-year
    C. 7-year
    D. 9-year

66. Office furniture and equipment, except computers, have a _____ recovery period for depreciation purposes.

    A. 3-year
    B. 5-year
    C. 7-year
    D. 9-year

67. Residential realty has a _____ recovery period for depreciation purposes.

    A. 20-year
    B. 27.5-year
    C. 31.5-year
    D. 39-year

68. Commercial realty has a _____ recovery period for depreciation purposes.

    A. 20-year
    B. 27.5-year
    C. 31.5-year
    D. 39-year

69. Several years ago, Tony purchased equipment for use in his business at a cost of $9,000. His cost recovery deductions totaled $4,574, and he later sold the equipment for $10,000. What is the amount of cost recovery deductions, if any, that must be recaptured?

    A. $1,000
    B. $4,574
    C. $5,574
    D. $9,000

The following information relates to questions 70 – 71.

Megan owns and operates Alpha Company as a sole proprietor. A few years ago, she purchased office furniture at a cost of $7,000 to use in her business. She used the straight-line method to recover the cost of the furniture, and she claimed $4,205 of cost recovery deductions. She sold the furniture this year for $12,600.

70. What is the amount of Section 1245 gain resulting from the sale?

    A. $2,520
    B. $2,795
    C. $6,840
    D. $7,010

71. What is the amount of Section 1231 gain resulting from the sale?

    A. $2,520
    B. $2,795
    C. $6,840
    D. $7,010

The following information relates to questions 72 – 74.

Kim owns machinery that has a fair market value of $55,000 and an adjusted basis of $17,000. Through an exchange, she acquires machinery from Mark that has a fair market value of $85,000 and an adjusted basis of $52,000. In the exchange, Kim pays Mark $30,000.

72. What is the amount of gain or loss, if any, realized by Kim in the exchange?

    A. $30,000
    B. $34,000
    C. $38,000
    D. $42,000

73. What is the amount of gain or loss, if any, recognized by Kim in the exchange?

    A. $0
    B. $17,000
    C. $30,000
    D. $38,000

74. What is Kim's substitute basis in the acquired property?

    A. $44,000
    B. $47,000
    C. $50,000
    D. $53,000

75. Erin reports the following transactions for the current year:

    1. Earned a salary of $90,000 through her full-time job.
    2. Schedule C loss of $8,000 (assume material participation).
    3. Received a $50,000 inheritance due to her father's death.

    What is Erin's gross income for the current year?

    A. $82,000
    B. $90,000
    C. $98,000
    D. $132,000

76. Laurie's jewelry collection was stolen from her home. The jewelry had a basis of $28,000 and was insured for $14,000. If the fair market value of the jewelry was $45,000, and Laurie's adjusted gross income is $52,000, what is the amount of Laurie's deductible casualty loss?

    A. $5,200
    B. $8,700
    C. $17,700
    D. $26,700

77. Richard and Sherry are recently divorced, and Sherry has custody of their 3-year-old son. Richard is required to pay Sherry $2,400 each month until their child reaches age 18, and then the payments decrease to $1,700 per month. The portion of each payment that Richard can deduct this year is:

    A. $0.
    B. $700.
    C. $1,700.
    D. $2,400.

78. **Which of the following is more beneficial to a taxpayer in a 28% bracket, a $4,000 deduction or a $1,000 credit?**

    A. The credit will benefit the taxpayer by an additional $120.
    B. The deduction will benefit the taxpayer by an additional $120.
    C. The deduction will benefit the taxpayer by an additional $300.
    D. The deduction and credit will benefit the taxpayer by the same amount.

79. **David purchased office furniture for his business for $4,300, and he paid $215 in sales tax. Assuming he uses MACRS, what is the cost recovery deduction for the first year?**

    A. $614
    B. $645
    C. $860
    D. $903

80. **Carol purchased a car for her business for $25,000. Assuming she uses MACRS, what is the cost recovery deduction for the first year?**

    A. $1,786
    B. $2,500
    C. $3,571
    D. $5,000

ANSWER KEY

1. A

For estimated tax payments, no penalty is imposed if a taxpayer did not have any income tax liability for the preceding year.

2. C

Step 1: $68,000 × 0.0765 = $5,202
Step 2: $68,000 − $5,202 = $62,798
Step 3: $62,798 × 0.1530 = $9,608

3. B

$180,000 × 0.5 = $90,000
Dan's overall charitable deduction is limited to 50% of AGI, or $90,000. Since the stock was held for less than one year, Dan's deduction is limited to the basis of $95,000. However, the 50% limit always applies, so only $90,000 can be deducted this year. The excess $5,000 is carried forward to next year.

4. B

$29,000 × 0.9 = $26,100
The required annual tax payment is the lesser of 90% of the current year's estimated tax bill, or 100% of last year's tax bill. If last year's tax return reported income over $150,000, Olivia would have to pay 110%, instead of 100%. The question states that Olivia expects her current year tax liability to be $29,000. Therefore, she can pay 90% of $29,000, equal to $26,100.

5. C

$73,000 + $40,000 = $113,000
William is permitted to deduct losses up to his basis of $113,000.

6. C

Last year's deduction = $97,280 × 0.5 = $48,640
This year's deduction = $51,200 − $48,640 = $2,560
Cash donations to qualified public charities are limited to 50% of the taxpayer's adjusted gross income. The excess amount can be carried forward to future years.

7. C

Step 1: Identify the investment income: $9,500
Step 2: 2% of AGI = $132,000 × 0.02 = $2,640
Step 3: $6,200 − $2,640 = $3,560
Step 4: $9,500 − $3,560 = $5,940

8. B

Portion of gain subject to capital gains tax = $390,000 − $320,000 = $70,000
The gain on the sale is not excluded because the couple did not own the house and use it as their principal residence during at least 2 of the last 5 years before the date of sale.

9. A
Portion of gain subject to capital gains tax = $0
The maximum exclusion of gain on the sale of a principal residence is $250,000 for single taxpayers who owned the house and used it as a principal residence during at least 2 of the last 5 years before the date of sale.

10. B
Step 1: Gain on sale = $450,000 – $175,000 = $275,000
Step 2: Portion of gain subject to capital gains tax = $275,000 – $250,000 = $25,000
The maximum exclusion of gain on the sale of a principal residence is $250,000 for single taxpayers who owned the house and used it as a principal residence during at least 2 of the last 5 years before the date of sale.

11. A
Portion of gain subject to capital gains tax = $0
The maximum exclusion of gain on the sale of a principal residence is $500,000 for married couples filing a joint tax return who owned the house and used it as their principal residence during at least 2 of the last 5 years before the date of sale.

12. C
Step 1: Monthly property tax = $1,740 / 6 months = $290
Step 2: The buyer will own the house for 4 months.
Step 3: Amount buyer owes seller = 4 months × $290 per month = $1,160

13. D
Step 1: Accumulated depreciation = 6 years × 0.045 per year = 0.27
Step 2: Original value = $255,000 / (1 – 0.27) = $349,315.07

14. B
Step 1: Accumulated depreciation = 12 years × 0.025 per year = 0.3
Step 2: Original value = $339,500 / (1 – 0.3) = $485,000

15. B
Depreciation = 1 / 27.5 years = 0.0364 = 3.64% per year

16. D
Economic life = 100% / 2% per year = 50 years

17. B
Step 1: Annual depreciation = 1 / 20 years = 0.05 per year
Step 2: Accumulated depreciation = 1 – ($372,000 / $620,000) = 0.4
Step 3: Number of years = 0.4 / 0.05 per year = 8 years

18. B
Step 1: Annual deprecation = 1 / 25 years = 0.04 per year
Step 2: Accumulated depreciation = 7 years × 0.04 = 0.28
Step 3: Value after 7 years = $410,000 × (1 – 0.28) = $295,200

19. D
Number of years = (1 − 0.3) / 0.035 per year = 20 years

20. B
Step 1: Annual depreciation = 1 / 25 years = 0.04 per year
Step 2: Accumulated depreciation = 1 − ($705,600 / $980,000) = 0.28
Step 3: Number of years = 0.28 / 0.04 per year = 7 years

21. C
Taxes owed from tax deduction = ($80,000 − $8,000) × 0.25 = $18,000

22. B
Taxes owed from tax credit = ($80,000 × 0.25) − $4,000 = $16,000

23. A
Step 1: Taxes owed from tax deduction = ($80,000 − $8,000) × 0.25 = $18,000
Step 2: Equivalent tax credit = ($80,000 × 0.25) − $18,000 = $2,000

24. A
$4,500 − $3,500 = $1,000 loss
Because Bill sold the property for a loss, the basis is the lesser of the fair market value ($4,500) or the original basis ($9,500).

25. B
Melissa's income is earned, so the kiddie tax rules don't apply. A child, under age 18, who is employed by a parent in an unincorporated business, does not have to pay Social Security taxes.

26. D
The purchase date (January 3rd) is within thirty days of the sale date (December 18th), and is considered a wash sale. This means that no loss deduction is allowed. The amount of the disallowed loss will be added to the cost basis of the shares that Joel purchased on January 3rd.

27. B
$3,200 − $2,800 = $400 net long-term capital gain

28. A
$3,500 − $800 = $2,700 net short-term capital loss

29. A
$2,700 − $400 = $2,300 net short-term capital loss

30. C
This is a bargain sale to charity. The taxable gain is calculated as follows:
Step 1: $225,000 (sale price) / $750,000 (FMV) = 30%
Step 2: 30% × $90,000 (basis) = $27,000
Step 3: $225,000 (sale price) − $27,000 = $198,000 taxable gain

31. D
Step 1: Total revenue = Total expenses + Net income
   Total revenue = $72,000 + $90,000 = $162,000
Step 2: Cash received from customers = Total revenue + Decrease in accounts receivable
   Cash received from customers = $162,000 + $12,000 = $174,000

32. C
Net profit margin = [Earnings before tax × (1 – t)] / Sales
Net profit margin = [0.193 × Sales × (1 – 0.38)] / Sales
Net profit margin = 0.193 × 0.62 = 0.1197 = 11.97%

33. B
Gain (or loss) on sale = Sale proceeds – (Acquisition cost – Accumulated depreciation)
–$400,000 = Sale proceeds – ($980,000 – $300,000)
Sale proceeds = $280,000

34. B
Step 1: Determine the per unit cost
   March 2016 purchase = $118,000 / 6,200 units = $19.03 per unit
   May 2016 purchase = $74,000 / 3,800 units = $19.47 per unit
Step 2: According to the FIFO method, the first 6,200 units sold came from the March purchase at $19.03 per unit. The next 1,300 units sold came from the May purchase at $19.47 per unit.
   $19.03 × 6,200 units = $117,986
   $19.47 × 1,300 units = $25,311
   $117,986 + $25,311 = $143,297

35. A
Step 1: ($118,000 + $74,000) / (6,200 units + 3,800 units) = $19.20
Step 2: $19.20 × 7,500 units = $144,000

36. B
Interest paid = Interest expense – Increase in interest payable
Interest paid = $2.47 million – $390,000 = $2.08 million

37. B
Taxes paid = Tax expense + Decrease in taxes payable
Taxes paid = $780,000 + $520,000 = $1.3 million

38. C
Cash paid to suppliers = Cost of goods sold + Increase in inventory – Increase in accounts payable
Cash paid to suppliers = $17.6 million + $1.1 million – $440,000 = $18.26 million

39. C
Step 1: $225,000 / $550,000 = 0.4091
Step 2: 0.4091 × $900,000 = $368,190

40. C

Gross profit = Revenue – Cost of goods sold
Gross profit = $51.5 million – $29.0 million = $22.5 million

41. B

Net income = Revenue – Expenses
Net income = $51.5 million – $29.0 million – $6.5 million – $1.1 million – $1.6 million
Net income = $13.3 million

42. D

Net revenue = Revenue – Returns and adjustments
Net revenue = $2,875,000 – $160,000 = $2,715,000

43. A

Annual depreciation expense = (Cost – Residual value) / Estimated useful life
Annual depreciation expense = ($490,000 – $20,000) / 8 years = $58,750

44. C

Step 1: Straight-line rate = 1/8 = 0.125
Step 2: Double declining rate = 0.125 × 2 = 0.25
Step 3: Depreciation = 0.25 × $490,000 = $122,500

45. A

According to the completed contract method, no revenue is reported until the project is completed.

46. B

Step 1: ($300,000 – $180,000) / $300,000 = 0.4
Step 2: 0.4 × $60,000 = $24,000

47. B

Cash received from customers = Revenue – Increase in accounts receivable
Cash received from customers = $800,000 – $90,000 = $710,000

48. B

Gain (or loss) on sale = Sale proceeds – (Acquisition cost – Accumulated depreciation)
Gain (or loss) on sale = $72,500 – {95,000 – [(($95,000 – $11,250) / 8 years) x 4 years]}
Gain (or loss) on sale = $72,500 – ($95,000 – $41,875) = $19,375

49. C

Step 1: Units in year-end inventory = Units available for sale – Units sold
      Units in year-end inventory = (60 + 24 + 126) – (18 + 49 + 84)
      Units in year-end inventory = 59
Step 2: According to the FIFO method, units from the October batch would remain in
      inventory: 59 units × $70 = $4,130

50. A
Step 1: Units in year-end inventory = Units available for sale – Units sold
Units in year-end inventory = (60 + 24 + 126) – (18 + 49 + 84)
Units in year-end inventory = 59
Step 2: According to the LIFO method, units from the February batch would remain in inventory: 59 units × $42 = $2,478

51. B
Gross profit margin = Gross profit / Revenue
Gross profit margin = $225,000 / $550,000 = 0.409 = 40.9%

52. B
Operating profit margin = Operating income / Revenue
Operating profit margin = $170,000 / $550,000 = 0.309 = 30.9%

53. A
Pretax margin = Earnings before taxes / Revenue
Pretax margin = $150,000 / $550,000 = 0.273 = 27.3%

54. B
Cash flow from operations = Net income + Depreciation – Increase in accounts receivable + Increase in accounts payable
Cash flow from operations = $660,000 + $35,000 – $110,000 + $120,000 = $705,000

55. A
Cash paid in salaries = Beg. salaries payable + Salaries expense – Ending salaries payable
Cash paid in salaries = $800,000 + $3.6 million – $500,000 = $3.9 million

56. A
Net cash flow from investing activities = –90,000 + $80,000 = –$10,000

57. B
Step 1: ($1,800,000 million – $1,200,000 million) / $1,800,000 million = 0.33$\overline{3}$
Step 2: 0.33$\overline{3}$ × $500,000 = $166,667

58. A
Theta Real Estate Company will not recognize any profit attributable to the down payment because the cash paid by the buyer does not exceed the original acquisition cost of $1.2 million.

59. B
The penalty for failing to pay taxes owed is 0.5% of the tax due, for each month or part of a month the tax remains unpaid, up to a maximum of 25%.

60. C
The penalty for failing to file a tax return is 5% of the unpaid taxes, for each month or part of a month that the tax return is late, up to a maximum of 25%.

61. A
$25,000 × 0.2 = $5,000
The penalty for underpayment of taxes due to negligence is 20%.

62. D
$10,000 \times 0.75 = \$7,500$
The penalty for underpayment of taxes due to civil fraud is 75%.

63. B
The penalty for a tax return preparer understating the amount of tax owed, not due to willful or reckless conduct, is the greater of $1,000 or 50% of the income derived by the tax return preparer with respect to the return or claim for refund.

64. B
Step 1: Penalty for negligence $= \$8,260 \times 0.2 = \$1,652$
Step 2: Penalty for civil fraud $= \$4,000 \times 0.75 = \$3,000$
Step 3: Total penalty $= \$1,652 + \$3,000 = \$4,652$

65. B
Cars, light-duty trucks, computers, and appliances have a 5-year recovery period for depreciation purposes.

66. C
Office furniture and equipment, except computers, have a 7-year recovery period for depreciation purposes.

67. B
Residential realty has a 27.5-year recovery period for depreciation purposes.

68. D
Commercial realty has a 39-year recovery period for depreciation purposes.

69. B
Step 1: $9,000 – $4,574 = $4,426
Step 2: $10,000 – $4,426 = $5,574
Step 3: The 1245 cost recovery recapture is the lesser of the cost recovery deductions taken ($4,574) or the gain realized ($5,574). The Section 1245 recapture is therefore $4,574.

70. B
Step 1: $7,000 – $4,205 = $2,795
Step 2: $12,600 – $2,795 = $9,805
Step 3: The 1245 cost recovery recapture is the lesser of the cost recovery deductions taken ($2,795) or the gain realized ($9,805). The Section 1245 recapture is therefore $2,795.

71. D
Step 1: $7,000 – $4,205 = $2,795
Step 2: $12,600 – $2,795 = $9,805
Step 3: The 1245 cost recovery recapture is the lesser of the cost recovery deductions taken ($2,795) or the gain realized ($9,805). The Section 1245 recapture is therefore $2,795.
Step 4: $9,805 – $2,795 = $7,010. This remaining gain is attributable to actual appreciation of the asset; therefore, there is $7,010 of Section 1231 gain.

72. C

$85,000 – $47,000 = $38,000

In the exchange, Kim received machinery with a fair market value of $85,000. She gave up an adjusted basis in her property of $17,000, plus $30,000 in cash, for a total of $47,000. The difference between $85,000 and $47,000 is the gain realized, $38,000.

Kim	Mark
FMV = $55,000	FMV = $85,000
Basis = $17,000	Basis = $52,000
Pays $30,000 to Mark	

73. A

The gain recognized is the lesser of the gain realized ($38,000) or boot received ($0).

74. B

$85,000 – $38,000 = $47,000

In the like-kind exchange, the substitute basis of the acquired asset is the fair market value of the asset acquired reduced by any gain realized but not recognized. In this scenario, the fair market value of the acquired asset is $85,000. There is $38,000 of gain realized but not recognized; therefore, $47,000 is the substitute basis in the acquired asset.

75. A

$90,000 – $8,000 = $82,000

Erin's salary of $90,000 is reduced by the $8,000 Schedule C loss. The inheritance is not included in Erin's gross income.

76. B

```
  $28,000  Basis
– $14,000  Insurance
–    $100  $100 floor
–  $5,200  10% of AGI
   $8,700  Casualty loss
```

77. C

Of the $2,400 payment, $1,700 is considered alimony and the other $700 is considered child support because it is tied to a contingency related to a minor child. Only alimony payments are deductible.

78. B

Step 1: $4,000 × 0.28 = $1,120
Step 2: $1,120 – $1,000 = $120

The deduction is more beneficial because it creates the equivalent of a $1,120 credit, which is $120 more than the $1,000 credit.

79. B

The office furniture is 7-year property.
($4,300 + $215) / 7 = $645

80. D

The car is 5-year property.
$25,000 / 5 = $5,000

SECTION 4

INVESTMENTS

QUESTIONS

1. Charles purchased a share of Theta stock for $184 and sold it for $173. If a $4.25 dividend was paid during the holding period, what was the total return?

   A. –4.67%
   B. –4.33%
   C. –4.02%
   D. –3.67%

2. Assume that Alpha stock pays a constant dividend of $4.10 per share each year. The dividend is not expected to grow. If an investor has a required rate of return of 7%, what is the intrinsic value of Alpha stock?

   A. $4.39 per share
   B. $17.07 per share
   C. $58.57 per share
   D. $69.10 per share

3. Based on the Markowitz model, which of the following securities would a rational investor select?

   A. Security A has a 5% rate of return and a beta of 0.8.
   B. Security B has a 6% rate of return and a beta of 0.8.
   C. Security C has a 3% rate of return and a beta of 0.7.
   D. Security D has a 6% rate of return and a beta of 0.6.

4. Sigma Investment Company has an 8.4% required rate of return. Their research analysts are researching a stock that is expected to pay a dividend of $5.15 per share. If the dividend is expected to increase by 3.3% each year, what is the current value of the stock?

   A. $98.78
   B. $99.24
   C. $100.98
   D. $102.12

5. Don purchased a bond with a face value of $1,000 and a coupon rate of 4.5%. His effective tax rate is 25%. If the risk-free rate is 4%, and coupon payments are made semiannually, what is the periodic interest payment?

   A. $16.88, paid twice per year
   B. $22.50, paid twice per year
   C. $45.00, paid once per year
   D. $45.00, paid twice per year

6. Kate purchases 100 shares of Beta stock for $60 per share with an initial margin of 50% and a 30% maintenance margin. At what share price will Kate receive a margin call?

    A. $41.75
    B. $42.86
    C. $43.65
    D. $44.40

7. Mary purchased a 5-year bond that pays a 3.5% semiannual coupon payment. The bond is priced at $97 per $100 of par value. What is the bond's current yield?

    A. 3.50%
    B. 3.61%
    C. 7.22%
    D. 7.65%

8. A stock with a beta of −1.2 and a standard deviation of 8.7 will change in which of the following ways if the stock market increases 4.5%?

    A. Increase by 2.8%
    B. Increase by 3.6%
    C. Decrease by 4.8%
    D. Decrease by 5.4%

9. A bond with a $1,000 face value has a current yield of 4.25%. If the bond pays a 4% coupon payment, what is the market price of the bond?

    A. $941.18
    B. $966.49
    C. $1,058.82
    D. $1,084.26

10. Assume the return on the stock market is 7.5% and the risk-free rate is 3.5%. What is the stock's risk premium if the beta is 0.7?

    A. 2.6%
    B. 2.8%
    C. 3.0%
    D. 3.2%

11. According to the Rule of 72, how many years will it take for an investment to double if the rate of return is 8% per year?

    A. 8 years
    B. 9 years
    C. 10 years
    D. 12 years

12. Security A has a standard deviation of 4.1% and Security B has a standard deviation of 9.3%. If the covariance of the returns is 19.37, what is the correlation coefficient?

    A. 0.452
    B. 0.508
    C. 0.571
    D. 0.614

13. A security has a coefficient of variation of 1.27 and a standard deviation of 13%. What is the expected return of the security?

    A. 10.236%
    B. 10.546%
    C. 10.690%
    D. 10.892%

14. Steven's portfolio has a mean return of 12%, a standard deviation of 6%, and a beta of 1.5. If the risk-free rate of return is 3%, what is the portfolio's Sharpe ratio?

    A. 0.5
    B. 1.5
    C. 2.0
    D. 6.0

15. The average annual return and the standard deviation of return for three investments is provided in the following table:

Investment	Average Annual Return (%)	Standard Deviation of Return (%)
Security A	6.8	2.2
Security B	2.1	1.3
Security C	4.4	1.2
Security D	5.2	1.6

    Based on the coefficient of variation, the riskiest investment is:

    A. Security A.
    B. Security B.
    C. Security C.
    D. Security D.

16. Katrina's portfolio has a Sharpe ratio of 0.55 and a mean return of 4.6%. If the 30-day T-bill rate is 2.0%, what is the standard deviation of return on Katrina's portfolio?

    A. 4.5%
    B. 4.6%
    C. 4.7%
    D. 4.8%

17. Assume that Security A has a standard deviation of 7.3% and Security B has a standard deviation of 11.2%. If the correlation coefficient between the two securities is 0.25, what is the covariance of the returns?

    A. 17.80
    B. 18.37
    C. 19.26
    D. 20.44

18. Jordan is researching two securities for possible inclusion in his portfolio. Security A has an expected return of 4% and a standard deviation of 9%. Security B has an expected return of 7% and a standard deviation of 11%. If Jordan is a risk-averse investor, he would select:

    A. Security A because it has a lower coefficient of variation.
    B. Security A because it has a higher coefficient of variation.
    C. Security B because it has a lower coefficient of variation.
    D. Security B because it has a higher coefficient of variation.

19. The following information has been provided for two funds an investor is researching:

Investment	Return	Beta
Kappa Fund	9%	1.1
Gamma Fund	14%	2.9

    If the risk-free rate is 3%, the difference in Treynor ratios between the two funds is:

    A. 1.66.
    B. 2.24.
    C. 2.87.
    D. 3.04.

20. Shelley's portfolio has a realized return of 7%. The realized return of the S&P 500 for the same time period is 6%, and the risk-free rate is 2%. If the beta of Shelley's portfolio is 0.75, what is the portfolio's alpha?

    A. −0.04
    B. −0.02
    C. 0.02
    D. 0.04

21. Zeta Fund has a Treynor ratio of 4.71. If the fund's return is 11%, and the risk-free rate is 2%, what is the fund's beta?

    A. 1.75
    B. 1.86
    C. 1.88
    D. 1.91

22. Richard, an investment manager, assembles the following portfolio consisting of two securities:

Security	Security Weight (%)	Expected Standard Deviation (%)
Security A	45	9
Security B	55	7

If the standard deviation of the portfolio is 7.9%, what is the covariance between the two securities?

A. 0.0019
B. 0.0063
C. 0.2475
D. 0.2794

The following information relates to questions 23 – 24.

An analyst provides the following information for an index comprised of four securities:

Security	Beginning of Period Price ($)	End of Period Price ($)
Security A	$38.00	$46.00
Security B	$29.00	$33.00
Security C	$50.00	$53.00
Security D	$80.00	$86.00

23. If the securities are part of an equal-weighted index, what is the return of the index?

A. 10.66%
B. 12.09%
C. 13.63%
D. 14.12%

24. If the securities are part of a price-weighted index, what is the return of the index?

A. 10.66%
B. 12.09%
C. 13.63%
D. 14.29%

25. Epsilon stock pays a constant dividend of $4 per share each year, and the dividend is not expected to increase. If the required rate of return is 9.5%, what is the current value of Epsilon stock?

A. $38.00
B. $40.00
C. $42.11
D. $44.97

26. Assume the next dividend for Omikron stock will be $2 per share, and investors require a 9% rate of return to purchase the stock. If the dividend increases by 4% each year, what is the current value of the stock?

A. $34.00
B. $36.00
C. $38.00
D. $40.00

27. If Delta Fund's Sharpe ratio is 0.76, its standard deviation is 9%, and the risk free-rate is 3.5%, what is the fund's return?

A. 9.92%
B. 10.34%
C. 10.56%
D. 10.72%

28. Linda, an investment analyst, is reviewing a security valued at $500,000 that pays 6.25% interest with two months remaining to maturity. What is the current value of the security?

A. $486,278.97
B. $490,413.17
C. $494,791.67
D. $498,372.28

29. A security has an expected return of 7.2% and a beta of 0.95. If the risk-free rate is 2.5%, then the expected return for the market, according to the capital asset pricing model, is:

A. 6.84%.
B. 7.45%.
C. 7.96%.
D. 8.02%.

30. A security has an expected annual return of 9.5% and an expected standard deviation of 14.4%. The market has an expected annual return of 7.8% and an expected standard deviation of 12.2. If the correlation between the security and the market is 0.75, what is the security's beta?

A. 0.64
B. 0.89
C. 1.02
D. 1.09

31. A share of Omega preferred stock has a par value of $100 and a preferred dividend rate of 6.25%. If the required return is 11.5%, what is the price per share?

    A. $54.35
    B. $98.50
    C. $184.00
    D. $196.00

The following information relates to questions 32 – 33.
Theta Holdings, a large multinational corporation, acquires Lambda Manufacturing Company for $40 million. As a result of the acquisition, Theta Holdings' standard deviation is reduced from 42% to 27%, and its correlation with the market decreases from 0.89 to 0.68. Assume the standard deviation and return of the market remains unchanged at 19% and 8%, respectively.

32. What was the beta of Theta Holdings before the acquisition?

    A. 1.86
    B. 1.91
    C. 1.93
    D. 1.97

33. What was the beta of Theta Holdings after the acquisition?

    A. 0.90
    B. 0.97
    C. 1.01
    D. 1.03

34. Jason believes the share price of Gamma stock will decrease in the short term. He has decided to sell short 500 shares at the current market price of $89. If the initial margin requirement is 35%, what amount must Jason contribute as margin?

    A. $15,575
    B. $22,250
    C. $28,925
    D. $30,485

35. Nicole sold short 25 shares of Epsilon stock at a price of $98.50 per share. She also simultaneously placed a "good-till-cancelled, stop 102, limit 107 buy" order. Excluding transaction costs, what is Nicole's maximum possible loss?

    A. $208.50
    B. $210.50
    C. $212.50
    D. $214.25

36. Alpha Corporation has an issue of 2.90%, $50 par value, perpetual, non-convertible, non-callable preferred shares outstanding. If the intrinsic value of a preferred share is $11.75, what is the required rate of return?

A. 10.92%
B. 11.86%
C. 12.34%
D. 13.08%

37. Sigma stock is currently selling at $44 per share, and Thomas has $8,000 to invest in the stock. However, he can borrow an additional $8,000 from his broker, and invest $16,000 total. If the maintenance margin is 35%, a margin call will first occur when Sigma stock reaches a price of:

A. $31.25.
B. $33.85.
C. $35.10.
D. $37.35.

38. Omikron LLC has an issue of 5.3%, $50 par value, perpetual, non-convertible, non-callable preferred shares outstanding. If the required rate of return is 6.25%, what is the intrinsic value of a preferred share?

A. $41.20
B. $42.40
C. $43.60
D. $44.10

39. An investment analyst provides the following information for Beta stock:

Number of shares outstanding	500,000
Expected constant dividend	$3.75 per share
Dividend growth rate	0%

If an investor's required rate of return is 8.5%, Beta stock's current share price is:

A. $41.10.
B. $42.36.
C. $43.07.
D. $44.12.

40. For the next three years, the annual dividends of Zeta stock are expected to be $1.50, $1.60, and $1.70. The stock price is expected to be $14.00 at the end of three years. If the required rate of return is 8%, what is the estimated price per share?

A. $14.67
B. $14.81
C. $15.23
D. $16.10

41. An investment analyst provides the following information for Epsilon stock:

Number of shares outstanding	1,200,000
Expected next dividend	$2.50 per share
Dividend growth rate (annual)	3%

If an investor's required rate of return is 9%, Epsilon stock's current share price is:

A. $40.35.
B. $41.67.
C. $42.20.
D. $43.33.

The following information relates to questions 42 – 44.

Theresa, an investment manager, anticipates that the price of a particular underlying stock, currently selling at $64, is going to increase in value over the next three months. She purchases a call option expiring in three months on the underlying stock. The call option has an exercise price of $68 and sells for $5.

42. If the price of the underlying stock is $71 in three months, what is Theresa's profit?

A. –$3
B. –$2
C. –$1
D. $0

43. If the price of the underlying stock is $73 in three months, what is Theresa's profit?

A. –$2
B. –$1
C. $0
D. $1

44. If the price of the underlying stock is $77 in three months, what is Theresa's profit?

A. $3
B. $4
C. $5
D. $6

45. Robert, a futures trader, takes a long position in a contract. The initial margin requirement is $9 and the maintenance margin requirement is $5. If he deposits the required initial margin on the trade date, and then the margin account balance drops to $3, what is the variation margin the following day?

A. $4
B. $5
C. $6
D. $7

46. Gamma Corporation provides the following information at its annual shareholder meeting:

Gross income	$2,300,000
Net income	$950,000
Number of shares outstanding	250,000
Price per share	$9.10
Average total book value of equity	$3,260,000
Total liabilities	$2,980,000

What is Gamma Corporation's return on equity (ROE)?

A. 27.72%
B. 29.14%
C. 31.88%
D. 33.59%

47. Theta Corporation provides the following information at its annual shareholder meeting:

Net sales	$425,000
Average total assets	$200,000
Average shareholders' equity	$180,000
Effective tax rate	35%

What is Theta Corporation's asset turnover?

A. 1.11
B. 2.13
C. 2.36
D. 2.85

48. Roger, an investment analyst, provides the following information regarding Kappa Corporation:

Number of shares outstanding	800,000
Earnings retention rate	35%
Dividend growth rate	4.5%
Effective Tax Rate	30%

What is Kappa Corporation's return on equity (ROE)?

A. 9.36%
B. 12.86%
C. 14.26%
D. 16.38%

49. Assume that an investment has a forward price of $16.52, the risk-free rate is 4%, and the contract expires in 3 months. What is the underlying price of the investment?

    A. $16.06
    B. $16.12
    C. $16.22
    D. $16.36

50. Patricia, an investment manager, bought a call option for $3.00. The option has a strike price of $37.00, and the stock is currently valued at $36.00. The call option would cost $2.50 if purchased today. Ignoring transaction costs, what is the intrinsic value of the option?

    A. –$0.50
    B. $0
    C. $1.00
    D. $2.00

51. An investor purchases two puts. The first is a September Delta put at $35, underlying currently selling at $37. The second is a November Omega put at $28, underlying currently selling at $25. Ignoring transaction costs, what is the value of the options?

    A. Delta: –$2; Omega: $3
    B. Delta: $0; Omega: –$3
    C. Delta: $0; Omega: $3
    D. Delta: $2; Omega: $3

52. Assume that an investment has an underlying price of $27, the risk-free rate is 2.5%, and the contract expires in 4 months. What is the forward price?

    A. $27.22
    B. $27.65
    C. $28.03
    D. $29.19

The following information relates to questions 53 – 58.
David, an investment manager, anticipates that the price of a particular underlying stock, currently selling at $184, is going to decrease in value over the next six months. He purchases a put option expiring in six months on the underlying stock. The put option has an exercise price of $177 and sells for $4.

53. If the price of the underlying stock is $190 in six months, what is David's profit?

    A. –$6
    B. –$5
    C. –$4
    D. –$3

54. If the price of the underlying stock is $184 in six months, what is David's profit?

    A. –$5
    B. –$4
    C. –$3
    D. –$2

55. If the price of the underlying stock is $174 in six months, what is David's profit?

    A. –$1
    B. $0
    C. $1
    D. $3

56. If the price of the underlying stock is $170 in six months, what is David's profit?

    A. $2
    B. $3
    C. $4
    D. $5

57. If the price of the underlying stock is $166 in six months, what is David's profit?

    A. $4
    B. $5
    C. $6
    D. $7

58. The maximum profit to the buyer and the maximum loss to the buyer, respectively, is:

    A. $4, $173.
    B. $173, $4.
    C. $173, ∞.
    D. ∞, $4.

The following information relates to questions 59 – 63.
A currency is selling for $1.23. A put option selling for $0.12 has an exercise price of $1.27. Consider the following questions about a protective put if the price at expiration is $1.32.

59. What is the value at expiration for the buyer?

    A. $1.27
    B. $1.30
    C. $1.32
    D. $1.36

60. What is the profit at expiration for the buyer?

A. –$0.05
B. –$0.03
C. $0.03
D. $0.05

61. What is the maximum loss to the buyer?

A. $0.03
B. $0.08
C. $0.12
D. ∞

62. What is the maximum profit to the buyer?

A. $0.08
B. $0.12
C. $0.27
D. ∞

63. What is the breakeven price of the currency at expiration?

A. $1.33
B. $1.34
C. $1.35
D. $1.36

The following information relates to questions 64 – 68.

A bond with a face value of $1,000 is selling for $965. A call option selling for $6 has an exercise price of $1,025. Consider the following questions about a covered call if the price of the bond at expiration is $1,040.

64. What is the value at expiration for the buyer?

A. $1,015
B. $1,020
C. $1,025
D. $1,035

65. What is the profit at expiration for the buyer?

A. $65
B. $66
C. $67
D. $68

66. What is the maximum profit to the buyer?

A. $65
B. $66
C. $67
D. ∞

67. What is the maximum loss to the buyer?

A. $959
B. $965
C. $1,000
D. ∞

68. What is the breakeven price of the bond at expiration?

A. $959
B. $965
C. $1,000
D. $1,025

69. Ruth owns an investment yielding an 18% pre-tax return. If she is in the 28% tax bracket, what is the equivalent after-tax return?

A. 5.04%
B. 12.96%
C. 14.28%
D. 23.04%

70. Josh owns an investment yielding an after-tax return of 9.5%. If he is in the 15% tax bracket, what is the equivalent pre-tax return?

A. 1.43%
B. 8.08%
C. 10.93%
D. 11.18%

The following information relates to questions 71 – 72.
Lambda Inc. provides the following information on their consolidated year-end financial statement:

Cash and cash equivalents	$150,000
Short-term marketable securities	$90,000
Receivables	$195,000
Other non-financial assets	$65,000
Current liabilities	$200,000
Non-current liabilities	$40,000

71. What is Lambda Inc.'s quick ratio?

    A. 2.08
    B. 2.18
    C. 2.50
    D. 2.72

72. What is Lambda Inc.'s cash ratio?

    A. 0.63
    B. 1.00
    C. 1.20
    D. 1.30

73. Alpha Inc. has a current ratio of 3.0 and a quick ratio of 2.5. If the company's current liabilities are $80,000, what is the amount of inventory?

    A. $20,000
    B. $40,000
    C. $60,000
    D. $80,000

74. Annual receivables / Sales per day = _____

    A. Fixed asset turnover ratio
    B. Return on equity
    C. Inventory turnover ratio
    D. Average collection period

75. Earnings before interest and taxes (EBIT) / Annual sales = _____

    A. Average collection period
    B. Quick ratio
    C. Net profit margin
    D. Operating profit margin

76. (Current assets – Inventory) / Current liabilities = _____

    A. Inventory turnover ratio
    B. Current ratio
    C. Quick ratio
    D. Return on assets

77. Earnings after taxes / Total assets = _____

    A. Net profit margin
    B. Return on assets
    C. Return on equity
    D. Current ratio

78. Current assets / Current liabilities = _____

   A. Quick ratio
   B. Current ratio
   C. Debt-to-equity ratio
   D. Return on assets

79. Earnings after taxes / Annual sales = _____

   A. Average collection period
   B. Quick ratio
   C. Operating profit margin
   D. Net profit margin

80. Earnings after taxes / Common stockholder equity = _____

   A. Net profit margin
   B. Return on equity
   C. Operating profit margin
   D. Current ratio

81. Ben purchased 100 shares of Theta stock for $55 per share. At the end of two years, he sold the shares for $60 per share. In the first year, the stock did not pay a dividend. In the second year, the stock paid a $4 dividend. What was the holding period return of Ben's investment?

   A. 9.09%
   B. 11.21%
   C. 13.46%
   D. 16.36%

82. Sigma Investment Company quotes an annual interest rate of 6.00%. If that rate is equal to an effective annual rate of 6.17%, then the investment company is compounding interest:

   A. daily.
   B. monthly.
   C. quarterly.
   D. semiannually.

83. In a normal distribution, the percent of observations that lie between plus and minus one standard deviation from the mean, plus and minus two standard deviations from the mean, and plus and minus three standard deviations from the mean, respectively, is:

   A. 50%, 68%, 95%.
   B. 68%, 95%, 99%.
   C. 75%, 95%, 99%.
   D. 95%, 98%, 99%.

84. Gary purchases a share of Zeta stock for $39.10 and receives a dividend of $1.05 one year later. If the share of stock is sold for $42.30 immediately following the dividend payment, what is the holding period return?

    A. 10.87%
    B. 11.21%
    C. 12.04%
    D. 12.27%

85. Catherine purchased an investment with a 250-day holding period yield (HPY) of 5.5%. What is the effective annual yield (EAY) on her investment?

    A. 6.79%
    B. 7.65%
    C. 7.98%
    D. 8.13%

86. Beta Corporation loans money at a quoted annual interest rate of 5.00%. If interest is compounded daily, what is the effective annual rate?

    A. 5.13%
    B. 5.47%
    C. 5.92%
    D. 6.02%

87. The Delta Fund has recorded the following investment returns since inception:

    2012: +9.1%
    2013: −1.3%
    2014: +2.1%
    2015: +10.1%
    2016: +13.1%

    What is the geometric mean for the Delta Fund?

    A. 4.64%
    B. 5.86%
    C. 6.48%
    D. 7.02%

88. Epsilon Fund has recorded the following investment returns for the past seven years: −3%, +4%, +5%, −3%, +2%, +6%, −1%. The mean, median, and mode of the returns, respectively, is:

    A. 1.43%, −3%, 2%.
    B. 1.43%, 2%, −3%.
    C. 2.86%, −3%, 2%.
    D. 2.86%, 2%, 4%.

89. An analyst is reviewing Kappa Corporation's earnings per share (EPS) and has recorded the following probability distribution for the upcoming fiscal year:

Probability	EPS ($)
0.25	3.00
0.25	3.10
0.50	3.20

What is the expected value of Kappa Corporation's EPS?

A. $3.09
B. $3.11
C. $3.13
D. $3.26

90. In 2016, an investor allocated her portfolio in the following asset classes:

Asset Class	Asset Allocation (%)	Asset Class Return (%)
Domestic equities	40.0	+10.0
International equities	20.0	−4.0
Corporate bonds	30.0	+6.0
Money market funds	10.0	+2.0

What is the portfolio's weighted average return for 2016?

A. 4.8%
B. 5.2%
C. 5.6%
D. 5.8%

91. Lisa owns a bond with a holding period yield (HPY) of 3.55%. If the face value of the bond is $1,000, what is the present value?

A. $961.50
B. $963.46
C. $965.72
D. $994.75

92. Monica purchased a share of Beta stock for $90.00 and sold it for $95.50. If the total return was 7.50%, the dividend paid during the holding period was:

A. $1.20.
B. $1.25.
C. $1.35.
D. $1.40.

93. Omega Corporation plans to borrow enough money to repurchase 80,000 shares of stock. The following information relates to the share repurchase:

Shares outstanding before buyback	2.5 million
Earnings per share before buyback	$2.25
Share price at time of buyback	$46.50
After-tax cost of borrowing	9%

What will be Omega Corporation's earnings per share (EPS) after the buyback?

A. $2.06
B. $2.19
C. $2.27
D. $2.36

94. George, an investment analyst, has provided the following information for two newly formed mutual funds:

Mutual Fund	Time Since Inception	Return Since Inception (%)
Gamma Fund	211 days	3.98
Lambda Fund	14 months	8.11

What is the difference in the annualized rate of return between the two mutual funds?

A. 0.07%
B. 0.12%
C. 0.17%
D. 0.24%

The following information relates to questions 95 – 96.
William, an investment manager, researches the historic geometric returns for the following asset classes:

Asset Class	Geometric Return (%)
Common stocks	7.2
High-yield bonds	5.8
T-bills	1.9
Inflation	3.3

95. What is the real rate of return for common stocks?

A. 3.78%
B. 4.49%
C. 5.20%
D. 6.05%

96. What is the real rate of return for high-yield bonds?

    A. 1.71%
    B. 2.42%
    C. 3.83%
    D. 4.22%

97. Johnathan, an investment analyst, has gathered the following data for Omikron Corporation:

Expected earnings per share	$4.80
Expected dividends per share	$1.90
Expected dividend growth rate	3.4% per year

If the required rate of return is 7.5%, what is the price/earnings multiple?

    A. 5.7
    B. 9.7
    C. 10.4
    D. 11.2

The following information relates to questions 98 – 99.
An analyst provides the following information for an index comprised of four securities:

	Beginning of period		End of period	
Security	Price ($)	Shares	Price ($)	Shares
Security A	$18.00	200	$20.00	200
Security B	$26.00	400	$24.00	400
Security C	$33.00	500	$39.00	500
Security D	$38.00	500	$42.00	500

98. If the securities are part of a price-weighted index, what is the price return?

    A. 7.9%
    B. 8.7%
    C. 9.3%
    D. 10.1%

99. If the securities are part of a value-weighted index, what is the return?

    A. 7.9%
    B. 8.7%
    C. 9.3%
    D. 10.1%

100. Zeta Manufacturing Corporation provides the following information for the fiscal year (in millions):

Net income	$1.5
Total sales	$4.0
Beginning of year total assets	$17.4
Beginning of year total liabilities	$12.4

What is Zeta Manufacturing Corporation's return on equity (ROE)?

A. 30%
B. 38%
C. 70%
D. 82%

ANSWER KEY

1. D

$R_t = (P_t - P_{t-1} + D_t) / P_{t-1}$

$R_t = (\$173 - \$184 + \$4.25) / \$184 = -0.0367 = -3.67\%$

2. C

Intrinsic value of Alpha stock = ($4.10 / 0.07) = $58.57 per share

3. D

Security D is the answer by process of elimination. Begin with the securities with a beta of 0.8 and select the one with the highest return. This eliminates security A. Next, compare the securities that have an investment return of 6% and select the one with the least risk (lowest beta). This eliminates security B. Finally, compare the two securities that remain, C and D. Security D provides a higher return for less risk than security C. Therefore, security D is the investment a rational investor would select.

4. C

$P_0 = D_1 / (r - g)$

$P_0 = \$5.15 / (0.084 - 0.033) = \$100.98$

5. B

Periodic interest payment = ($1,000 × 0.045) / 2 = $22.50

6. B

Step 1: 100 shares × $60 per share = $6,000

Step 2: $6,000 – $3,000 equity = $3,000 margin

Step 3: $3,000 / 0.7 = $4,286

Step 4: $4,286 / 100 shares = $42.86 per share

7. B

Current yield = Sum of coupon payments / Market price

Current yield = ($100 × 0.035) / $97 = 0.0361 = 3.61%

8. D

4.5% × –1.2 = –5.4%

A stock with a beta of –1.2 will move 120% in the opposite direction of the market. If the stock market increases by 4.5%, the stock will decrease by 5.4%.

9. A

Current yield = Sum of coupon payments / Market price

0.0425 = $40 / Market price

Market price = $941.18

10. B

(7.5% – 3.5%) × 0.7 = 2.8%

The stock's risk premium is the part of the capital asset pricing model (CAPM) equation located inside the parentheses, multiplied by the stock's beta.

11. B

72 / 8 = 9 years

By dividing 72 by the annual interest rate, an investor can determine how many years it will take for the initial investment to double.

12. B

$Cov = \rho_{AB} \times \sigma_A \times \sigma_B$

$19.37 = \rho_{AB} \times 4.1 \times 9.3$

$\rho_{AB} = 0.508$

13. A

$CV = s / \overline{X}$

$1.27 = 13\% / \overline{X}$

$\overline{X} = 10.236\%$

14. B

$$S_h = \frac{R_p - R_f}{S_p}$$

$$S_h = \frac{12\% - 3\%}{6\%} = 1.5$$

15. B

$CV = s / \overline{X}$

$CV_A = 2.2\% / 6.8\% = 0.32$

$CV_B = 1.3\% / 2.1\% = \underline{0.62}$

$CV_C = 1.2\% / 4.4\% = 0.27$

$CV_D = 1.6\% / 5.2\% = 0.31$

Security B has the highest coefficient of variation, which implies the greatest level of dispersion around the mean.

16. C

$$S_h = \frac{R_p - R_f}{S_p}$$

$$0.55 = \frac{4.6\% - 2\%}{S_p}$$

$S_p = 4.7\%$

17. D

$Cov = \rho_{AB} \times \sigma_A \times \sigma_B$

$Cov = 0.25 \times 7.3 \times 11.2 = 20.44$

18. C

$CV = s / \overline{X}$

$CV_A = 9\% / 4\% = 2.25$

$CV_B = 11\% / 7\% = 1.57$

A risk-averse investor would select Security B because it has a lower coefficient of variation.

19. A

$$\text{Treynor} = \frac{R_P - R_f}{\beta_P}$$

$$\text{Treynor}_{\text{Kappa}} = \frac{9\% - 3\%}{1.1} = 5.45$$

$$\text{Treynor}_{\text{Gamma}} = \frac{14\% - 3\%}{2.9} = 3.79$$

Difference = 5.45 – 3.79 = 1.66

20. C

$\alpha_p = R_p - [R_f + \beta_p(R_m - R_f)]$
$\alpha_p = 0.07 - [0.02 + 0.75(0.06 - 0.02)] = 0.02$

21. D

$$\text{Treynor} = \frac{R_P - R_f}{\beta_P}$$

$$4.71 = \frac{11\% - 2\%}{\beta_P}$$

$\beta_P = 1.91$

22. B

Step 1: Weighted average = $W_A R_A + W_B R_B$
    Weighted average = $(0.45 \times 0.09) + (0.55 \times 0.07) = 0.079 = 7.9\%$
    Because the standard deviation (7.9%) equals the weighted average, the correlation between the securities is 1.0.
Step 2: Cov = $\rho_{AB} \times \sigma_A \times \sigma_B$
    Cov = $1.0 \times 0.09 \times 0.07 = 0.0063$

23. B

An equal-weighted index applies the same weight (1/4) to each security's return.
Step 1: Find the return of each security
    r_A = ($46 – $38) / $38 = 0.2105 = 21.05%
    r_B = ($33 – $29) / $29 = 0.1379 = 13.79%
    r_C = ($53 – $50) / $50 = 0.0600 = 6.00%
    r_D = ($86 – $80) / $80 = 0.0750 = 7.50%
Step 2: (1/4) × (21.05% + 13.79% + 6.00% + 7.50%) = 12.09%

24. A

The price return of a price-weighted index is the percentage change in price of the index.
Step 1: $38 + $29 + $50 + $80 = $197
Step 2: $46 + $33 + $53 + $86 = $218
Step 3: ($218 – $197) / $197 = 0.1066 = 10.66%

25. C

$P_0 = D_1 / (r - g)$
$P_0 = \$4 / (0.095) = \$42.11$

26. D
$P_0 = D_1 / (r - g)$
$P_0 = \$2 / (0.09 - 0.04) = \$40.00$

27. B
$$S_h = \frac{R_p - R_f}{S_p}$$

$$0.76 = \frac{R_p - 3.5\%}{9\%}$$

$R_p = 10.34\%$

28. C
Current value $= \$500,000 - [0.0625 \times (2/12) \times \$500,000]$
Current value $= \$500,000 - \$5,208.33 = \$494,791.67$

29. B
$E(R_i) = R_f + \beta_i[E(R_m) - R_f]$
$7.2\% = 2.5\% + 0.95[E(R_m) - 2.5\%]$
$E(R_m) = 7.45\%$

30. B
$B_i = (\rho_{i,m} \times \sigma_i) / \sigma_m$
$B_i = (0.75 \times 0.144) / 0.122 = 0.89$

31. A
$$P_p = \frac{D_p}{r_p}$$

$$P_p = \frac{0.0625 \times \$100}{0.115} = \$54.35$$

32. D
$B_i = (\rho_{i,m} \times \sigma_i) / \sigma_m$
$B_i = (0.89 \times 0.42) / 0.19 = 1.97$

33. B
$B_i = (\rho_{i,m} \times \sigma_i) / \sigma_m$
$B_i = (0.68 \times 0.27) / 0.19 = 0.97$

34. A
Step 1: 500 shares $\times$ \$89 per share $= \$44,500$
Step 2: \$44,500 $\times$ 35% $= \$15,575$

35. C
Step 1: \$107 - \$98.50 $= \$8.50$
Step 2: \$8.50 per share $\times$ 25 shares $= \$212.50$

36. C

$V_0 = D_0 / r$

$\$11.75 = (\$50 \times 0.029) / r$

$r = 0.1234 = 12.34\%$

37. B

$$\frac{\text{Equity/share}}{\text{Price/share}} = \frac{(0.50)(\$44) + P - \$44}{P} = 35\%$$

$P = \$33.85$

38. B

$V_0 = D_0 / r$

$V_0 = (\$50 \times 0.053) / 0.0625 = \$42.40$

39. D

$P_0 = D_1 / (r - g)$

$P_0 = \$3.75 / 0.085 = \$44.12$

40. C

$$V_0 = \frac{D_1}{(1+r)^1} + \frac{D_2}{(1+r)^2} + \frac{D_3}{(1+r)^3} + \frac{P_3}{(1+r)^3}$$

$$V_0 = \frac{\$1.50}{(1.08)^1} + \frac{\$1.60}{(1.08)^2} + \frac{\$1.70}{(1.08)^3} + \frac{\$14.00}{(1.08)^3}$$

$V_0 = \$1.389 + \$1.372 + \$1.350 + \$11.114 = \$15.23$

41. B

$P_0 = D_1 / (r - g)$

$P_0 = \$2.50 / (0.09 - 0.03) = \$41.67$

42. B

Step 1: Value at expiration $= \max(0, S_T - X)$

   Value at expiration $= \max(0, \$71 - \$68) = \$3$

Step 2: Profit $= c_T - c_0$

   Profit $= \$3 - \$5 = -\$2$

43. C

Step 1: Value at expiration $= \max(0, S_T - X)$

   Value at expiration $= \max(0, \$73 - \$68) = \$5$

Step 2: Profit $= c_T - c_0$

   Profit $= \$5 - \$5 = \$0$

44. B

Step 1: Value at expiration $= \max(0, S_T - X)$

   Value at expiration $= \max(0, \$77 - \$68) = \$9$

Step 2: Profit $= c_T - c_0$

   Profit $= \$9 - \$5 = \$4$

45. C
When the balance in the margin account falls below the maintenance margin, Robert must deposit funds to return the balance to the initial margin requirement. Therefore, the variation margin is $9 – $3 = $6.

46. B
$ROE_t = NI_t / Average BVE_t$
$ROE_t = \$950{,}000 / \$3{,}260{,}000 = 0.2914 = 29.14\%$

47. B
Asset turnover = Net sales / Average total assets
Asset turnover = $425,000 / $200,000 = 2.13

48. B
g = Earnings retention rate × ROE
0.045 = 0.35 × ROE
ROE = 0.1286 = 12.86%

49. D
Forward price $= S_0(1 + r)^T$
$\$16.52 = S_0(1.04)^{(3/12)}$
$S_0 = \$16.36$

50. B
The call option is out-of-the-money because the strike price ($37.00) exceeds the market price ($36.00). Therefore, the value of the option is $0.

51. C
The Delta option is out-of-the-money, therefore its value is $0.
The value of the Omega option is $28 – $25 = $3.

52. A
Forward price $= S_0(1 + r)^T$
Forward price $= \$27(1.025)^{(4/12)} = \$27.22$

53. C
Step 1: Value at expiration $= max(0, X – S_T)$
Value at expiration $= max(0, \$177 – \$190) = \$0$
Step 2: Profit $= p_T – p_0$
Profit $= \$0 – \$4 = –\$4$

54. B
Step 1: Value at expiration $= max(0, X – S_T)$
Value at expiration $= max(0, \$177 – \$184) = \$0$
Step 2: Profit $= p_T – p_0$
Profit $= \$0 – \$4 = –\$4$

55. A
Step 1: Value at expiration = $\max(0, X - S_T)$
      Value at expiration = $\max(0, \$177 - \$174) = \$3$
Step 2: Profit = $p_T - p_0$
      Profit = $\$3 - \$4 = -\$1$

56. B
Step 1: Value at expiration = $\max(0, X - S_T)$
      Value at expiration = $\max(0, \$177 - \$170) = \$7$
Step 2: Profit = $p_T - p_0$
      Profit = $\$7 - \$4 = \$3$

57. D
Step 1: Value at expiration = $\max(0, X - S_T)$
      Value at expiration = $\max(0, \$177 - \$166) = \$11$
Step 2: Profit = $p_T - p_0$
      Profit = $\$11 - \$4 = \$7$

58. B
Maximum profit to the buyer = $X - p_0 = \$177 - \$4 = \$173$
Maximum loss to the buyer = $\$4$

59. C
$V_T = S_T + \max(0, X - S_T)$
$V_T = \$1.32 + \max(0, \$1.27 - \$1.32) = \$1.32$

60. B
Profit = $V_T - (S_0 + p_0)$
Profit = $\$1.32 - (\$1.23 + \$0.12) = -\$0.03$

61. B
Maximum loss to the buyer = $S_0 + p_0 - X$
Maximum loss to the buyer = $\$1.23 + \$0.12 - \$1.27 = \$0.08$

62. D
The maximum profit is unlimited.

63. C
$S_T^* = S_0 + p_0$
$S_T^* = \$1.23 + \$0.12 = \$1.35$

64. C
$V_T = S_T - \max(0, S_T - X)$
$V_T = \$1,040 - \max(0, \$1,040 - \$1,025)$
$V_T = \$1,040 - \$15 = \$1,025$

65. B
Profit = $V_T - (S_0 - c_0)$
Profit = $\$1,025 - (\$965 - \$6) = \$66$

66. B

Maximum profit to the buyer $= X - S_0 + c_0$

Maximum profit to the buyer $= \$1,025 - \$965 + \$6 = \$66$

67. A

Maximum loss to the buyer $= S_0 - c_0$

Maximum loss to the buyer $= \$965 - \$6 = \$959$

68. A

$S_T^* = S_0 - c_0$

$S_T^* = \$965 - \$6 = \$959$

69. B

After-tax return $= 0.18 \times (1 - 0.28) = 12.96\%$

70. D

Pre-tax return $= 0.095 / (1 - 0.15) = 11.18\%$

71. B

Quick ratio $=$ (Cash + Short-term marketable securities + Receivables) / Current liabilities

Quick ratio $= (\$150,000 + \$90,000 + \$195,000) / \$200,000$

Quick ratio $= \$435,000 / \$200,000 = 2.18$

72. C

Cash ratio $=$ (Cash + Short-term marketable securities) / Current liabilities

Cash ratio $= (\$150,000 + \$90,000) / \$200,000$

Cash ratio $= \$240,000 / \$200,000 = 1.20$

73. B

Step 1: Current ratio $=$ Current assets / Current liabilities

$3.0 =$ Current assets / $\$80,000$

Current assets $= \$240,000$

Step 2: Quick ratio $=$ (Current assets – Inventory) / Current liabilities

$2.5 = (\$240,000 -$ Inventory$) / \$80,000$

Inventory $= \$40,000$

74. D

Annual receivables / Sales per day $=$ Average collection period

75. D

Earnings before interest and taxes (EBIT) / Annual sales $=$ Operating profit margin

76. C

(Current assets – Inventory) / Current liabilities $=$ Quick ratio

77. B

Earnings after taxes / Total assets $=$ Return on assets

78. B
Current assets / Current liabilities = Current ratio

79. D
Earnings after taxes / Annual sales = Net profit margin

80. B
Earnings after taxes / Common stockholder equity = Return on equity

81. D
HPR = [($6,000 + $400) – $5,500] / $5,500
HPR = $900 / $5,500 = 0.1636 = 16.36%

82. B
The investment company is compounding interest monthly.
EAR = (1 + Periodic interest rate)^m – 1
EAR = [1 + (0.06 / 12)]^{12} – 1
EAR = 1.0617 – 1 = 0.0617 = 6.17%

83. B
In a normal distribution, 68% of observations lie between plus and minus one standard deviation from the mean, 95% lie between plus and minus two standard deviations from the mean, and 99% lie between plus and minus three standard deviations from the mean.

84. A
HPR = $(P_1 - P_0 + D_1)$ / P_0
HPR = ($42.30 – $39.10 + $1.05) / $39.10 = 0.1087 = 10.87%

85. D
EAY = (1 + HPY)$^{365/t}$ – 1
EAY = (1.055)$^{365/250}$ – 1
EAY = 1.081306 – 1 = 0.0813 = 8.13%

86. A
EAR = (1 + Periodic interest rate)^m – 1
EAR = [1 + (0.05 / 365)]^{365} – 1
EAR = 1.0513 – 1 = 0.0513 = 5.13%

87. C
G = [$(X_1)(X_2)(X_3)...(X_N)$]$^{1/N}$ – 1
G = [(1 + 0.091) × (1 – 0.013) × (1 + 0.021) × (1 + 0.101) × (1 + 0.131)]$^{(1/5)}$ – 1
G = (1.091 × 0.987 × 1.021 × 1.101 × 1.131)$^{(1/5)}$ – 1
G = (1.369)$^{(1/5)}$ – 1 = 0.0648 = 6.48%

88. B
Mean = [(–3%) + (4%) + (5%) + (–3%) + (2%) + (6%) + (–1%)] / 7 = 1.43%
Median = –3%, –3%, –1%, +2%, +4%, +5%, +6% = 2%
Mode = –3% is the only number that appears twice, therefore it is the mode.

89. C
$E(X) = P(X_1)X_1 + P(X_2)X_2 + P(X_3)X_3$
$EPS = (0.25 \times \$3.00) + (0.25 \times \$3.10) + (0.50 \times \$3.20)$
$EPS = \$0.75 + \$0.775 + \$1.60 = \$3.125 = \$3.13$

90. B
$R_p = w_1R_1 + w_2R_2 + w_3R_3 + w_4R_4$
$R_p = (0.40 \times 0.10) + (0.20 \times -0.04) + (0.30 \times 0.06) + (0.10 \times 0.02)$
$R_p = 0.04 - 0.008 + 0.018 + 0.002 = 0.052 = 5.2\%$

91. C
$FV_N = PV(1 + r)^N$
$\$1,000 = PV(1.0355)$
$PV = \$965.72$

92. B
$R_t = (P_t - P_{t-1} + D_t) / P_{t-1}$
$0.075 = (\$95.50 - \$90.00 + D_t) / \$90.00$
$D_t = \$1.25$

93. B
Step 1: Total earnings before buyback: $2.25 per share $\times$ 2,500,000 shares = $5,625,000
Step 2: Total amount borrowed: $46.50 per share $\times$ 80,000 shares = $3,720,000
Step 3: After-tax cost of borrowing: $3,720,000 $\times$ 0.09 = $334,800
Step 4: Shares after buyback: 2,500,000 shares – 80,000 shares = 2,420,000 shares
Step 5: EPS after buyback: ($5,625,000 – $334,800) / 2,420,000 shares = $2.19 per share

94. A
$r_{annual} = (1 + r_{period})^c - 1$
$r_{Gamma} = (1.0398)^{365/211} - 1 = 0.0698 = 6.98\%$
$r_{Lambda} = (1.0811)^{12/14} - 1 = 0.0691 = 6.91\%$
Difference = 6.98% – 6.91% = 0.07%

95. A
$(1 + r_{real}) = (1 + r) / (1 + \pi)$
$(1 + r_{real}) = 1.072 / 1.033$
$r_{real} = 1.0378 - 1 = 0.0378 = 3.78\%$

96. B
$(1 + r_{real}) = (1 + r) / (1 + \pi)$
$(1 + r_{real}) = 1.058 / 1.033$
$r_{real} = 1.0242 - 1 = 0.0242 = 2.42\%$

97. B
$$\frac{P_0}{E_1} = \frac{D_1 / E_1}{r - g}$$

$$\frac{P_0}{E_1} = \frac{1.90 / 4.80}{0.075 - 0.034} = 9.7$$

98. B
The price return of a price-weighted index is the percentage change in price of the index.
Step 1: $18 + $26 + $33 + $38 = $115
Step 2: $20 + $24 + $39 + $42 = $125
Step 3: ($125 – $115) / $115 = 0.087 = 8.7%

99. C
The return of a value-weighted index is the percentage change in market value over the period.
Step 1: ($18 × 200 shares) + ($26 × 400 shares) + ($33 × 500 shares) + ($38 × 500 shares) = $49,500
Step 2: ($20 × 200 shares) + ($24 × 400 shares) + ($39 × 500 shares) + ($42 × 500 shares) = $54,100
Step 3: ($54,100 – $49,500) / $49,500 = 0.093 = 9.3%

100. A
$ROE_t = NI_t / \text{Average } BVE_t$
$ROE_t = \$1.5 / (\$17.4 - \$12.4) = 0.3 = 30\%$

SECTION 5

RETIREMENT PLANNING

QUESTIONS

1. Elle, a retiree, would like to receive Social Security benefits 36 months before her full retirement age. By what percentage will her benefit be reduced?

   A. 10%
   B. 15%
   C. 20%
   D. 25%

2. Alpha Corporation has a defined benefit pension plan, and its pension obligation is $4.4 million at the end of the plan year. The company has $3.3 million in pension assets. According to US GAAP, Alpha Corporation's balance sheet would show a net pension obligation of:

   A. $1.1 million.
   B. $2.2 million.
   C. $3.3 million.
   D. $4.4 million.

3. Matt, age 35, needs to take a $7,000 hardship withdrawal from his 401(k). He will incur a _____ premature distribution penalty.

   A. $0
   B. $700
   C. $1,400
   D. $3,500

4. Last year, Rick contributed $7,000 to his IRA when the contribution limit was only $5,500. His excess contribution is subject to an excise tax of:

   A. $75.
   B. $90.
   C. $350.
   D. $420.

5. Beta Corporation has 140 employees. All employees are covered by the company's defined benefit plan except for 80 associates. Has the minimum participation requirement been met for the defined benefit plan?

   A. Yes, both parts of the 50/40 test have been met.
   B. Yes, but only one part of the 50/40 test has been met.
   C. No, neither part of the 50/40 test has been met.
   D. No, only one part of the 50/40 test has been met and the plan must pass both tests.

6. Theta Corp. currently has 45 employees. What is the maximum number of additional employees the company can hire and still be permitted to maintain a SIMPLE plan?

   A. 25 employees
   B. 45 employees
   C. 55 employees
   D. 100 employees

7. A premature distribution from a qualified plan, SEP, or IRA will incur a _____ penalty.

   A. 5%
   B. 10%
   C. 15%
   D. 20%

8. Pursuant to a divorce decree, Devin, age 40, is required to transfer $120,000 from his qualified retirement plan to an IRA in the name of his ex-spouse. The transfer will be subject to which of the following penalties?

   A. $0
   B. $12,000
   C. $18,000
   D. Ordinary income tax rates

9. According to required minimum distribution rules, Ralph was supposed to distribute $36,000 last year, but failed to do so. He is required to pay an excise tax of:

   A. $3,600.
   B. $9,000.
   C. $18,000.
   D. $27,000.

10. If a defined benefit plan is top heavy, the minimum contribution the employer must make on behalf of non-key employees is equal to the lesser of _____ , or _____ per year of service, of each non-key employee's average compensation for the five highest consecutive years.

    A. 10%; 2%
    B. 10%; 3%
    C. 20%; 2%
    D. 20%; 3%

11. Jill has earned 4 quarters of coverage during the last 9 calendar quarters. To be considered "currently insured" for Social Security benefits, she must earn at least _____ additional quarters of coverage during the next _____ calendar quarters.

    A. 2; 4
    B. 2; 5
    C. 3; 5
    D. 3; 6

12. April withdrew money from her IRA 21 days ago to make a first-time home purchase. For the distribution to be considered penalty-free, she has _____ remaining to use the money towards the home purchase.

    A. 9 days
    B. 39 days
    C. 69 days
    D. 99 days

13. For determining eligibility to receive Social Security retirement benefits, what is the maximum number of credits that can be earned in a single calendar year?

    A. 2 credits
    B. 4 credits
    C. 6 credits
    D. 8 credits

14. For Social Security benefits, which of the following is the full retirement age for an individual born in the year 1937 or earlier?

    A. Age 64
    B. Age 65
    C. Age 66
    D. Age 67

The following information relates to questions 15 – 16.
Sigma Corporation recently adopted a defined benefit plan with a base percentage of 22.50%.

15. What is the maximum permitted disparity for the plan?

    A. 22.50%
    B. 26.25%
    C. 45.00%
    D. 52.50%

16. Given the permitted disparity, what is the excess percentage?

    A. 22.50%
    B. 26.25%
    C. 45.00%
    D. 52.50%

17. George's primary insurance amount (PIA) for Social Security is $612. If his wife's PIA is $1,434, what is George's spousal PIA?

    A. $612
    B. $717
    C. $1,224
    D. $1,434

18. In a defined contribution plan, the premiums paid for whole life insurance coverage cannot exceed _____ of the contributions made to the plan on a participant's behalf, and the premiums paid for term, universal, or variable life insurance cannot exceed _____ of the contributions made to the plan on a participant's behalf.

    A. 10%; 25%
    B. 25%; 50%
    C. 50%; 25%
    D. 75%; 50%

19. James is employed by a university, has not previously made contributions to a 403(b) plan, and currently has 3 years of service. How many additional years of service must James achieve to be eligible for the special catch-up provision?

    A. 2 years
    B. 7 years
    C. 12 years
    D. 17 years

20. Through the first six months of the year, Alec has purchased stock with a fair market value of $8,000 through his employee stock purchase plan (ESPP). How much additional stock is he permitted to purchase through his ESPP before the end of the calendar year?

    A. $2,000
    B. $17,000
    C. $42,000
    D. $92,000

21. Kathy earned $1,800 working part-time in 2018. How many Social Security credits has she earned?

   A. 1 credit
   B. 2 credits
   C. 3 credits
   D. 4 credits

22. If a defined contribution plan is top heavy, what is the minimum contribution the employer must make on behalf of non-key employees?

   A. 2%
   B. 3%
   C. 4%
   D. 5%

23. Nick, age 53, recently quit his job. He would like to distribute money from his 401(k) but wants to avoid any penalties related to the distribution. If he waits a minimum of _____ years, his distribution will not be subject to the _____ premature distribution penalty.

   A. 2; 10%
   B. 2; 15%
   C. 6; 15%
   D. 6; 20%

24. For a defined contribution plan, annual contributions to an employee's account are limited to the lesser of _____ of compensation or _____ in 2018.

   A. 20%; $18,500
   B. 20%; $24,500
   C. 25%; $55,000
   D. 25%; $220,000

25. Employer contributions to a defined contribution plan must use either the _____ cliff vesting or _____ graded vesting schedules.

   A. 3-year; 6-year
   B. 3-year; 7-year
   C. 5-year; 6-year
   D. 5-year; 7-year

26. Employer contributions to a defined benefit plan must use either the _____ cliff vesting or _____ graded vesting schedules.

   A. 3-year; 6-year
   B. 3-year; 7-year
   C. 5-year; 6-year
   D. 5-year; 7-year

27. Aaron will take a $15,000 distribution from his 401(k) before the end of the year to purchase a new car. He is 58 years old and recently retired from his job. Assuming that he is in the 25% tax bracket, he will have to pay a _____ premature distribution penalty.

    A. $0
    B. $1,500
    C. $3,750
    D. $5,000

28. Tony is a participant in his employer's defined benefit plan. If his projected retirement benefit is $850 per month, then how much life insurance on Tony's life can the plan trustee apply for?

    A. $8,500
    B. $10,000
    C. $50,000
    D. $85,000

29. To pass the percentage test, Beta Corp.'s qualified retirement plan must benefit at least what percentage of all employees who are not highly compensated?

    A. 50%
    B. 60%
    C. 70%
    D. 80%

The following information relates to questions 30 – 31.
Delta Manufacturing Corporation recently adopted a defined contribution plan with a base percentage of 6.5%.

30. What is the maximum permitted disparity for the plan?

    A. 5.7%
    B. 6.5%
    C. 11.4%
    D. 12.2%

31. Given the permitted disparity, what is the excess percentage?

    A. 5.7%
    B. 6.5%
    C. 11.4%
    D. 12.2%

32. For a SIMPLE IRA, the employer must match dollar for dollar the first _____ of compensation that eligible employees elect to defer, or the employer must make annual non-elective contributions equal to _____ of compensation for all eligible employees.

   A. 2%; 3%
   B. 2%; 4%
   C. 3%; 2%
   D. 4%; 3%

33. Bret, age 35, has been a plan participant in his employer's SIMPLE IRA for one year. If he makes a withdrawal of $8,000 this year, he will be subject to a/an _____ early withdrawal penalty.

   A. $0
   B. $800
   C. $2,000
   D. $4,000

34. Angela, age 35, has been a plan participant in her employer's SIMPLE 401(k) for one year. If she makes a withdrawal of $8,000 this year, she will be subject to a/an _____ early withdrawal penalty.

   A. $0
   B. $800
   C. $2,000
   D. $4,000

35. Next year, Jessica plans to retire after working for Gamma Corporation for 23 years. Upon retiring, Jessica will receive a monthly pension equal to 3.1% of her final-average monthly salary ($8,000) multiplied by her total years of service. If the unit-benefit formula caps the level of service at 25 years, what will Jessica's income replacement ratio be?

   A. 22.5%
   B. 28.7%
   C. 71.3%
   D. 77.5%

36. Social Security benefits are reduced by _____ of 1% for each month before full retirement age that a fully insured worker retires, up to _____ months.

   A. 5/9; 24
   B. 5/9; 36
   C. 5/12; 24
   D. 5/12; 36

37. Epsilon Corporation provides its retired employees with a pension equal to 2.5% of final-average earnings per year for up to 25 years of service. If Ben has worked for Epsilon Corporation for 29 years and had final-average earnings of $90,000, how much will his pension be if he retires when he reaches 30 years of service?

   A. $22,500
   B. $33,750
   C. $56,250
   D. $67,500

38. John has accumulated 28 quarters of coverage (credits) throughout his working career. To be deemed "fully insured" by Social Security, he will need to accumulate how many additional credits?

   A. 12 credits
   B. 22 credits
   C. 33 credits
   D. 42 credits

The following information relates to questions 39 – 40.
Renee, age 30, is an employee of Zeta Corporation. She participates in the company's 401(k), which uses a 2 to 6-year graded vesting schedule. Renee has been employed with the company for 4 full years.

39. What percentage of Renee's salary deferrals are vested?

   A. 40%
   B. 60%
   C. 80%
   D. 100%

40. What percentage of the employer contributions in Renee's 401(k) are vested?

   A. 40%
   B. 60%
   C. 80%
   D. 100%

41. David, a Vice President at Theta Corporation, earns $450,000 in 2018. If the company has installed a 15% money purchase plan, how much can the company contribute on his behalf?

   A. $18,500
   B. $41,250
   C. $55,000
   D. $67,250

42. Jennifer is a fully insured worker. If she retires more than _____ months before her full retirement age, her Social Security benefit will be reduced by _____ of 1% per month.

    A. 24; 5/8
    B. 24; 5/12
    C. 36; 5/8
    D. 36; 5/12

43. Shelley, age 53, is an employee of Omikron LLC. The maximum amount that she can contribute to a SIMPLE IRA in 2018, and the maximum amount that she can borrow from the plan, respectively, is:

    A. $12,500, $0
    B. $12,500, $10,000
    C. $15,500, $0
    D. $15,500, $10,000

44. Michael, the owner of Kappa Corporation, has installed an integrated profit sharing plan. If the company's annual payroll is $680,000, what is the maximum contribution that Michael can make in 2018?

    A. $55,000
    B. $120,000
    C. $136,000
    D. $170,000

45. Colin, age 58, contributes to his employer's 401(k). In 2018, he will contribute $24,500 to the plan through salary deferrals, and he would like to contribute to an IRA as well. If he is single and his income is $250,000, the maximum IRA contribution that he can make is:

    A. $5,500 to a deductible IRA.
    B. $6,500 to a deductible IRA.
    C. $6,500 to a non-deductible IRA.
    D. $6,500 to a Roth IRA.

46. Ann, age 53, owns Omega Corporation. Her annual salary is $600,000, and her company has 120 employees. How much can she contribute to an IRA in 2018?

    A. $0
    B. $5,500
    C. $6,000
    D. $6,500

47. Jerry, a retiree, would like to receive Social Security benefits 12 months before his full retirement age. By what percentage will his benefit be reduced?

    A. 6.67%
    B. 13.33%
    C. 20.00%
    D. 25.00%

48. Megan, age 58, earns an annual salary of $125,000 and participates in her employer's 401(k) and money purchase plans. If the employer contribution to the money purchase plan is 10% of salary, then her maximum combined retirement plan contribution in 2018 will be:

    A. $30,500.
    B. $33,000.
    C. $37,500.
    D. $38,000.

49. Dominic, age 44, is an employee of Lambda Corporation. He earns an annual salary of $84,000 and participates in the company's 401(k), which matches 50% of employee contributions, up to 5%. If Dominic makes the maximum 401(k) contribution in 2018, how much will he receive through the company match?

    A. $2,100
    B. $4,200
    C. $18,500
    D. $22,700

The following information relates to questions 50 – 51.
Gene has contributed $34,000 to his 401(k) through salary deferrals over the last several years. In addition, his employer has provided $9,000 through matching contributions.

50. If Gene is 40% vested, how much can he borrow from the plan today?

    A. $10,000
    B. $18,800
    C. $37,600
    D. $43,000

51. If Gene had not received matching contributions from his employer, how much could he borrow from the plan today?

    A. $10,000
    B. $17,000
    C. $18,800
    D. $34,000

52. Cynthia, age 57, has been a teacher in the Lincoln County School District for 20 years. What is the maximum contribution she can make to her 403(b) in 2018?

A. $18,500
B. $24,500
C. $27,500
D. $28,000

53. Josephine and Walter are a married couple who will both reach full retirement age next year. When they apply for Social Security benefits, they will each be entitled to receive a benefit based on the greater of their own retirement benefit or _____ of their spouse's benefit.

A. 25%
B. 50%
C. 75%
D. 100%

54. Mary Beth, age 51, and Anthony, age 47, are a married couple who would like to make IRA contributions for 2018. If Mary Beth will earn $200,000 this year, and Anthony expects to have no earned income, the maximum deductible IRA contributions they can make are:

A. $0 for Mary Beth and $0 for Anthony.
B. $6,500 for Mary Beth and $0 for Anthony.
C. $6,500 for Mary Beth and $5,500 for Anthony.
D. $6,500 for Mary Beth and $6,500 for Anthony.

The following information relates to questions 55 – 56.
Cindy is granted a non-qualified stock option (NQSO) that provides her with the right to purchase 1,000 shares of company stock for $10 per share. Assume Cindy's ordinary income tax rate is 28% and the capital gains rate is 15%.

55. How much will Cindy owe in taxes if she exercises the option when the stock's fair market value is $20 per share?

A. $0
B. $1,500
C. $2,800
D. $3,000

56. How much will Cindy owe in taxes if she sells the stock for $30 per share after holding for two years?

A. $0
B. $1,500
C. $2,800
D. $3,000

The following information relates to questions 57 – 59.
Thomas's employer, Omikron Corporation, has granted him an incentive stock option (ISO) that provides him with the right to purchase 1,000 shares of company stock for $10 per share. Assume that Thomas's ordinary income tax rate is 28% and the capital gains rate is 15%.

57. How much will Thomas owe in taxes if he exercises the option when the stock's fair market value is $20 per share?

    A. $0
    B. $1,500
    C. $2,800
    D. $3,000

58. How much will Thomas owe in taxes if he sells the stock for $30 per share after holding for two years?

    A. $0
    B. $1,500
    C. $2,800
    D. $3,000

59. How much will Thomas owe in taxes if he sells the stock for $40 per share after holding for two years?

    A. $0
    B. $3,000
    C. $4,500
    D. $6,000

60. Three years ago, Stan was granted incentive stock options (ISOs) by his employer. How many remaining years does Stan have to exercise the options?

    A. 2 years
    B. 7 years
    C. 12 years
    D. 17 years

ANSWER KEY

1. C
Step 1: $5/9 \times 0.01 = 0.005556$
Step 2: 0.005556×36 months $= 0.2 = 20\%$
Elle's benefit will be reduced by 20%, which is equal to 5/9 of 1% for each month that Social Security benefits are taken early.

2. A
Net pension obligation = Pension obligation – Pension assets
Net pension obligation = $4.4 million – $3.3 million = $1.1 million

3. B
$7,000 \times 0.1 = \$700$
Hardship withdrawals taken from a 401(k) are subject to a 10% premature distribution penalty.

4. B
Step 1: $7,000 – $5,500 = $1,500
Step 2: $1,500 \times 0.06 = \$90$
If an individual contributes more to an IRA than is permitted, the excess contribution is subject to a 6% excise tax.

5. A
The minimum participation requirement has been satisfied because the plan covers at least the lesser of 50 employees (140 – 80 = 60) or 40% of all employees (140 × 40% = 56).

6. C
100 employees – 45 employees = 55 employees
In order to maintain a SIMPLE plan, an employer may not have more than 100 employees.

7. B
A premature distribution from a qualified plan, SEP, or IRA will incur a 10% penalty.

8. A
Amounts transferred from a qualified retirement plan to an IRA of a spouse or former spouse pursuant to a divorce decree are not subject to a penalty, regardless of age.

9. C
$36,000 \times 0.5 = \$18,000$
There is an excise tax of 50% on the amount that should have been distributed from a retirement plan according to required minimum distribution rules but was not distributed during the year.

10. C
If a defined benefit plan is top heavy, the minimum contribution the employer must make on behalf of non-key employees is equal to the lesser of 20%, or 2% per year of service, of each non-key employee's average compensation for the five highest consecutive years.

11. A
Step 1: 6 quarters – 4 quarters = 2 quarters
Step 2: 13 quarters – 9 quarters = 4 quarters
A worker is considered "currently insured" for Social Security benefits if he or she has earned at least 6 quarters of coverage during the previous 13 calendar quarters.

12. D
120 days – 21 days = 99 days
Penalty-free distributions from an IRA for a first-time home purchase must be used within 120 days of the money being withdrawn.

13. B
For determining eligibility to receive Social Security retirement benefits, a maximum of 4 credits (quarters of coverage) may be earned in a single calendar year.

14. B
For Social Security benefits, full retirement age for an individual born in the year 1937 or earlier is age 65.

15. A
The maximum permitted disparity in a defined benefit plan is the lesser of the base percentage (22.50%) or 26.25%.

16. C
The maximum permitted disparity in a defined benefit plan is the lesser of the base percentage (22.50%) or 26.25%. The excess percentage is 22.50% + 22.50% = 45.00%.

17. B
George's spousal PIA is the greater of his PIA ($612) or 50% of his wife's PIA ($1,434 × 50% = $717).

18. C
In a defined contribution plan, the premiums paid for whole life insurance coverage cannot exceed 50% of the contributions made to the plan on a participant's behalf, and the premiums paid for term, universal, or variable life insurance cannot exceed 25% of the contributions made to the plan on a participant's behalf.

19. C
15 years – 3 years = 12 years
A special catch-up provision is permitted in 403(b) plans for employees with at least 15 years of service who have not made contributions and are employed by universities.

20. B
$25,000 – $8,000 = $17,000
The maximum fair market value of stock an employee has the right to purchase through an employee stock purchase plan (ESPP) cannot exceed $25,000 in any calendar year.

21. A
The amount of earnings needed to earn one Social Security credit in 2018 is $1,320. Therefore, Kathy has earned one credit.

22. B
If a defined contribution plan is top heavy, then the minimum contribution the employer must make on behalf of non-key employees is 3%.

23. A
55 years – 53 years = 2 years
Distributions from a 401(k) following separation from service after age 55 are not subject to the 10% premature distribution penalty.

24. C
For a defined contribution plan, annual contributions to an employee's account are limited to the lesser of 25% of compensation or $55,000 in 2018.

25. A
Employer contributions to a defined contribution plan must use either the 3-year cliff vesting or 6-year graded vesting schedules.

26. D
Employer contributions to a defined benefit plan must use either the 5-year cliff vesting or 7-year graded vesting schedules.

27. A
Distributions from a 401(k) following separation from service after attaining age 55 are not subject to the 10% premature distribution penalty. The question asks about the *premature distribution penalty* that Aaron will pay, not the taxes that he will owe on the distribution.

28. D
$850 × 100 = $85,000
In a defined benefit plan, an insurance benefit must not be greater than 100 times the expected monthly retirement income benefit. Therefore, if the participant's expected benefit is $850 per month, the plan trustee can apply for $85,000 of insurance on the participant's life.

29. C
For a qualified retirement plan to pass the percentage test, the plan must benefit at least 70% of all employees who are not highly compensated.

30. A
The maximum permitted disparity in a defined contribution plan is the lesser of the base percentage (6.5%) or 5.7%.

31. D
The maximum permitted disparity in a defined contribution plan is the lesser of the base percentage (6.5%) or 5.7%. The excess percentage is 6.5% + 5.7% = 12.2%.

32. C
For a SIMPLE IRA, the employer must match dollar for dollar the first 3% of compensation that eligible employees elect to defer, or the employer must make annual non-elective contributions equal to 2% of compensation for all eligible employees.

33. C

$8,000 \times 25\% = \$2,000$

Early withdrawals from a SIMPLE IRA are subject to a 25% penalty if the withdrawals are made during the first two years of plan participation. After the initial two-year period, the early withdrawal penalty is reduced to 10%.

34. B

$8,000 \times 10\% = \$800$

The 25% early withdrawal penalty does not apply to SIMPLE 401(k) plans. For SIMPLE 401(k) plans, the early withdrawal penalty is 10%.

35. C

Income replacement ratio = 23 years × 3.1% per year = 71.3%

36. B

Social Security benefits are reduced by 5/9 of 1% for each month before full retirement age that a fully insured worker retires, up to 36 months.

37. C

Step 1: 25 years × 2.5% per year = 62.5%
Step 2: 62.5% × $90,000 = $56,250

38. A

40 credits – 28 credits = 12 credits

A worker is considered "fully insured" for Social Security benefits if he or she has earned at least 40 quarters of coverage (credits). Therefore, John needs to accumulate 12 additional credits.

39. D

Employee salary deferrals are always fully vested.

40. B

Vested employer contributions = 3 years × 20% per year = 60%

41. B

$275,000 × 15% = $41,250

The maximum contribution is limited by the annual compensation limit for 2018, which is $275,000.

42. D

If a fully insured worker retires more than 36 months early, the Social Security benefit is reduced by 5/12 of 1% per month.

43. C

$12,500 + $3,000 = $15,500

Employee contributions are limited to $12,500 in 2018. An additional $3,000 may be contributed by employees age 50 or older. Loans from IRAs are not permitted.

44. D

$680,000 × 25% = $170,000

The maximum contribution is limited to 25% of covered payroll.

45. C
Because Colin is an active participant in an employer sponsored retirement plan, he is subject to an AGI phaseout of $63,000 to $73,000 in 2018. Because his income is above the phaseout range, he is not eligible to make a deductible IRA contribution. His AGI is too high to contribute to a Roth IRA, as well. The Roth IRA AGI phaseout is $120,000 to $135,000 in 2018.

46. D
There is no indication that Omega Corporation offers a retirement plan to its employees, therefore Ann is not subject to an AGI phaseout for deducting her IRA contribution. She can contribute $6,500, which includes her $1,000 catch-up contribution for being age 50 or older.

47. A
Step 1: $5/9 \times 0.01 = 0.005556$
Step 2: 0.005556×12 months $= 0.0667 = 6.67\%$
Jerry's benefit will be reduced by 6.67%, which is equal to 5/9 of 1% for each month that Social Security benefits are taken early.

48. C
Step 1: Money purchase plan contribution $= \$125,000 \times 10\% = \$12,500$
Step 2: 401(k) contribution $= \$18,500 + \$6,000$ catch-up $= \$24,500$
Step 3: Combined contributions $= \$12,500 + \$24,500 = \$37,000$

49. A
Company match $= \$84,000 \times 50\% \times 5\% = \$2,100$

50. B
Step 1: Vested employer contributions $= \$9,000 \times 40\% = \$3,600$
Step 2: Total vested amount $= \$34,000 + \$3,600 = \$37,600$
Step 3: Maximum loan amount $= \$37,600 \times 50\% = \$18,800$
A loan from a 401(k) cannot exceed $50,000 or 50% of the participant's vested benefit. If the vested amount is $10,000 or less, the entire amount can be made available for loan without regard to the percentage restriction. Gene is 100% vested in his contributions.

51. B
$\$34,000 \times 50\% = \$17,000$
A loan from a 401(k) plan cannot exceed $50,000 or 50% of the participant's vested benefit. If the vested amount is $10,000 or less, the entire amount can be made available for loan without regard to the percentage restriction. Gene is 100% vested in his contributions.

52. C
$\$18,500 + \$6,000 + \$3,000 = \$27,500$
Cynthia is permitted a $6,000 catch-up contribution for being age 50 or older, and an additional $3,000 catch-up contribution for having 15 or more years of service with her current employer.

53. B
For married couples, each spouse is entitled to receive a Social Security benefit based on the greater of his or her own retirement benefit, or 50% of the spouse's benefit.

54. C

Mary Beth can contribute $6,500 to an IRA because she is age 50 or older, and a spousal IRA contribution of $5,500 can be made for Anthony. There is no catch-up contribution permitted for Anthony because he is not age 50 or older. Because there is no mention of an employer-sponsored retirement plan, they can deduct the contributions without regard to income limits.

55. C

Step 1: ($20 – $10) × 1,000 shares = $10,000
Step 2: $10,000 × 28% = $2,800

56. B

Step 1: ($30 – $20) × 1,000 shares = $10,000
Step 2: $10,000 × 15% = $1,500

57. A

No tax is paid (AMT preference item).

58. D

Step 1: ($30 – $10) × 1,000 shares = $20,000
Step 2: $20,000 × 15% = $3,000

59. C

Step 1: ($40 – $10) × 1,000 shares = $30,000
Step 2: $30,000 × 15% = $4,500

60. B

10 years – 3 years = 7 years
Incentive stock options (ISOs) cannot be exercised more than 10 years from the date of grant.

SECTION 6

ESTATE PLANNING

QUESTIONS

1. Howard dies owning Alpha stock, which is thinly traded. The nearest trading dates for Alpha stock were 3 days before the valuation date and 5 days after the valuation date. The mean price of the stock 3 days before the valuation date was $19, and the mean price 5 days after the valuation date was $20. What is the reportable value of Alpha stock in Howard's gross estate?

   A. $18.72
   B. $19.38
   C. $19.64
   D. $19.88

2. In a joint tenancy between non-spouses, what percentage of property will be included in the gross estate of the decedent unless the survivor shows consideration furnished?

   A. 0%
   B. 25%
   C. 50%
   D. 100%

3. Which of the following limits is imposed on direct charitable contributions made at death?

   A. Direct charitable contributions are limited to 10% of the decedent's gross estate.
   B. Direct charitable contributions are limited to 50% of the decedent's gross estate.
   C. Direct charitable contributions are limited to 75% of the decedent's gross estate.
   D. Direct charitable contributions can be made at death without limit.

4. Cliff gives stock worth a total of $60,000 in equal shares to his three daughters. Cliff's basis in the stock was $36,000. What is each daughter's basis in the stock she now owns?

   A. $8,000
   B. $12,000
   C. $20,000
   D. $60,000

5. For a charitable remainder trust, the payout rate stated in the trust cannot be less than _____ or more than _____ of the initial fair market value of the trust's assets.

   A. 5%; 25%
   B. 5%; 50%
   C. 10%; 25%
   D. 10%; 50%

6. Tyler inherited shares of Beta stock that are currently valued at $850,000. To retire and maintain his lifestyle, he requires a fixed 6% payout for life. Which of the following trusts will allow Tyler to achieve his goal?

A. CRUT
B. CRAT
C. CLAT
D. CLUT

7. A trust is established and funded with an initial gift of $175,000, and Crummey powers are attached to the trust. If the beneficiary chooses to exercise her demand right in 2018, how much money can she withdraw during the first thirty days?

A. $0
B. $5,000
C. $15,000
D. $175,000

8. Michelle wants to set up an irrevocable trust for her nephew, Paul. Michelle plans to gift $8,000 to the trust and attach Crummey powers. If Paul chooses to exercise his demand right in 2018, how much can he withdraw during the first thirty days?

A. $0
B. $5,000
C. $8,000
D. $15,000

9. Anneliese owned shares of Sigma stock with a basis of $40 per share. At the time of her death, the stock was worth $55 per share. Six months later, the stock had appreciated to a value of $65 per share. What is the basis of the stock in the hands of Anneliese's beneficiaries?

A. $15 per share
B. $40 per share
C. $55 per share
D. $65 per share

10. Len's adjusted gross estate is valued at $2,000,000. To qualify for the Section 6166 election, Len's interest in a closely-held business must exceed:

A. $500,000.
B. $700,000.
C. $900,000.
D. $1,000,000.

Rick and Gina
Statement of Financial Position
December 31, 20XX

ASSETS

		LIABILITIES AND NET WORTH		

Cash/Cash Equivalents

			Liabilities		
Checking account (R)[1]	$	4,000	1st mortgage on home[3]	$	83,000
Savings account (R)		55,000	Home equity loan		19,000
Money market fund (G)		21,000	Credit card balance[4]		33,000
			Car loans		28,000

Invested Assets

Value mutual fund (JT)	$	300,000	**TOTAL LIABILITIES**		$ 163,000
Common stocks (R)		395,000			

Retirement Assets

401(k) (R)	$	275,000
Profit sharing plan (G)		35,000

NET WORTH $1,320,000

Use Assets

House (JT)	$	280,000
Personal property (JT)[2]		56,000
Cars (JT)		62,000

TOTAL ASSETS $1,483,000

---

1. R = Rick as owner, G = Gina as owner, JT = Joint tenants with rights of survivorship
2. Includes jewelry valued at $25,000
3. 30-year fixed rate mortgage; principal amount last year was $86,200
4. 11.99% APR

11. If Rick dies this year, what will be the value of his gross estate for federal estate tax purposes?

A. $1,078,000
B. $1,113,000
C. $1,134,000
D. $1,256,000

12. Bob and Jean are married and own their home joint tenants with rights of survivorship. If Bob were to die, what percentage of the home would be included in his gross estate?

A. 0%
B. 50%
C. 100%
D. It depends on the amount of contributions made by Jean.

13. Richard and Daniel are brothers who own a parcel of land joint tenants with rights of survivorship. If Richard were to die, what percentage of the parcel of land would be included in his gross estate?

A. 0%
B. 50%
C. 75%
D. It depends on the amount of contributions made by Daniel.

14. Hillary's adjusted gross estate is valued at $3,000,000. To qualify for the Section 2032A "special use valuation," the net value of real property used in her family farming operation must be at least:

A. $750,000.
B. $1,050,000.
C. $1,350,000.
D. $1,500,000.

15. Sid's adjusted gross estate is valued at $1,500,000. To qualify for the Section 2032A "special use valuation," the net value of real and personal property used in his family farming operation must be at least:

A. $375,000.
B. $525,000.
C. $675,000.
D. $750,000.

16. Which of the following is the maximum reduction permitted to a decedent's gross estate under Section 2032A in 2018?

A. $890,000
B. $1,000,000
C. $1,040,000
D. $1,140,000

17. William and Maria are a married couple who live in a community property state. They purchased their home with joint funds after getting married. If Maria were to die and the house were to pass to William, what percentage of the home's value would be included in her gross estate?

A. 0%
B. 50%
C. 100%
D. It depends on the amount of contributions made by William.

18. Tim and Kristen are a married couple who own their home tenancy by entirety. If Tim were to die, what percentage of the home would be included in his gross estate?

    A. 0%
    B. 50%
    C. 100%
    D. It depends on the amount of contributions made by Kristen.

19. For property held as tenancy in common, what percentage of the property is included in the decedent's gross estate?

    A. 0%
    B. 50%
    C. 100%
    D. Fractional ownership

The following information relates to questions 20 – 21.
The executor provides the following information for a decedent's estate:

Gross estate	$3,400,000
Debts	$800,000
Funeral expenses	$10,000
Casualty and theft losses	$30,000
State death tax	$45,000
Marital deduction	$800,000
Charitable deduction	$650,000
Gift taxes paid on post-1976 gifts	$75,000
Generation-skipping transfer tax	$200,000

20. What is the value of the decedent's adjusted gross estate?

    A. $2,320,000
    B. $2,485,000
    C. $2,515,000
    D. $2,600,000

21. What is the value of the decedent's taxable estate?

    A. $980,000
    B. $1,065,000
    C. $1,120,000
    D. $1,290,000

22. As part of the estate tax calculation, Taxable estate + Adjusted taxable gifts = _____

    A. Tentative tax base
    B. Tentative tax
    C. Adjusted gross estate
    D. Net estate tax

23. As part of the estate tax calculation, Net estate tax + GSTT = _____

    A. Net estate tax
    B. Tentative tax
    C. Adjusted gross estate
    D. Total estate tax

24. As part of the estate tax calculation, Tentative tax base × Estate tax rate = _____

    A. Taxable estate
    B. Adjusted gross estate
    C. Tentative tax
    D. Net estate tax

25. To qualify for the Section 303 redemption, the stock's value must exceed what percentage of the decedent's adjusted gross estate?

    A. 15%
    B. 25%
    C. 35%
    D. 45%

26. For a charitable remainder trust, the present value of the remainder interest that passes to charity must be at least what percentage of the value of the property placed in the trust?

    A. 5%
    B. 10%
    C. 25%
    D. 50%

27. In 2018, Karen gifts property equally to her three children, valued at $175,000 per gift. If her husband agrees to split the gifts, how much gift tax will Karen be required to pay when she files her gift tax return? Assume this is the first year she's made a gift.

    A. $0
    B. $441,000
    C. $483,000
    D. $525,000

28. Mary and Steve, a wealthy married couple, would like to give the maximum amount possible to a single donee in 2018 without having to pay federal gift tax. If neither of them have used any portion of their unified credit before this year, what is the maximum amount they can give?

    A. $30,000
    B. $2,030,000
    C. $10,030,000
    D. $11,230,000

29. Bill is interested in reducing the size of his gross estate by selling shares of stock to charity. If the stock's basis is $44,000, and its value today is $57,300, what is Bill's taxable gain if he sells the stock for $44,000?

A. $9,357.19
B. $9,824.72
C. $10,212.91
D. $13,300.00

30. George purchased a condo with his daughter, and they each paid half of the $130,000 purchase price. They titled the condo joint tenants with rights of survivorship but kept no records related to the purchase. If George dies when the condo is worth $160,000, what amount will be included in his gross estate?

A. $65,000
B. $80,000
C. $130,000
D. $160,000

31. Louis purchased a house for $1,000,000 and transferred it to a qualified personal residence trust (QPRT) that was to continue for a term of 10 years. At the time the QPRT was created, the value of the house was $500,000. If Louis dies 8 years later when the house is valued at $1,600,000, what amount will be included in his gross estate?

A. $800,000
B. $1,000,000
C. $1,280,000
D. $1,600,000

The following information relates to questions 32 – 33.
Tom and Alison are a married couple who own their house in joint tenancy. Alison purchased the house several years ago for $230,000, using her own funds. In 2018, when the home is worth $350,000, Tom dies.

32. What amount will be included in Tom's gross estate?

A. $0
B. $115,000
C. $175,000
D. $350,000

33. What is Alison's new basis in the house when Tom dies?

A. $230,000
B. $260,000
C. $290,000
D. $350,000

34. Jessica is an income beneficiary of a trust with assets of $500,000. She also has a 5 by 5 power. If she dies this year before exercising the 5 by 5 power, what amount will be included in her gross estate?

    A. $0
    B. $5,000
    C. $25,000
    D. $500,000

The following information relates to questions 35 – 37.
Austin gifts shares of Epsilon common stock valued at $93,000 to his son, Jim. Austin purchased the stock several years ago for $47,000. Assume the stock has not paid any dividends and the basis has not changed.

35. What is the amount of Austin's taxable gift?

    A. $0
    B. $32,000
    C. $46,000
    D. $78,000

36. What is Jim's adjusted basis in the stock?

    A. $0
    B. $47,000
    C. $79,000
    D. $93,000

37. If Jim sells the stock for $117,000 a few years later, what is his taxable gain?

    A. $47,000
    B. $70,000
    C. $79,000
    D. $117,000

The following information relates to questions 38 – 39.
In 2018, Caleb gave his nephew, Robert, property with a basis of $1,200,000. The fair market value of the property on the date of transfer was $660,000.

38. What is the amount of Caleb's taxable gift?

    A. $645,000
    B. $660,000
    C. $1,185,000
    D. $1,200,000

39. What are the tax consequences if Robert sells the property for $600,000 three years later?

A. $60,000 loss
B. $540,000 loss
C. $600,000 loss
D. No gain or loss will be recognized.

The following information relates to questions 40 – 41.
Tony purchased a house several years ago for $450,000. In 2018, he gifted the house to his son, Devin, when it was valued at $575,000. Assume this is the first gift Tony has made.

40. How much gift tax will Tony be required to pay?

A. $0
B. $15,000
C. $125,000
D. $435,000

41. If Devin sells the house for $625,000, what is the amount of the taxable gift from Tony to Devin?

A. $50,000
B. $435,000
C. $560,000
D. $610,000

The following information relates to questions 42 – 43.
Carl and Ruth, a married couple, have always lived in a community property state. At the time of Carl's death, they owned $600,000 of community property, all of which was titled solely in Carl's name. They originally paid $450,000 for the property.

42. What amount will be included in Carl's gross estate?

A. $300,000
B. $450,000
C. $525,000
D. $600,000

43. What is Ruth's basis in the community property after Carl's death?

A. $300,000
B. $450,000
C. $525,000
D. $600,000

The following information relates to questions 44 – 45.
One year ago, Gretchen transferred stock valued at $200,000 to a trust for the benefit of her children. She paid gift tax of $60,000.

44. If Gretchen dies this year, what amount will be included in her gross estate?

   A. $0
   B. $60,000
   C. $200,000
   D. $260,000

45. If the transfer was made to Gretchen's husband instead of the trust, what amount would be included in her gross estate?

   A. $0
   B. $186,000
   C. $100,000
   D. $200,000

46. Steve made a $30,000 gift of a future interest to Kate in 2018. Assuming Steve is married, how much of the gift will qualify for the gift tax annual exclusion?

   A. $0
   B. $15,000
   C. $28,000
   D. $30,000

47. Tony gifted stock valued at $28,000 (basis of $20,000) to his cousin, Charles. Three years later, Charles gifts the stock, now worth $35,000, to his brother, Jerry. What is Jerry's basis?

   A. $7,000
   B. $15,000
   C. $20,000
   D. $35,000

48. Andrew and Linda, a married couple, purchased a house for $180,000. They titled the house joint tenants with rights of survivorship. Earlier this year, Andrew died when the house was valued at $320,000. What amount will be included in Andrew's gross estate?

   A. $90,000
   B. $140,000
   C. $160,000
   D. $320,000

49. Larry donated a house that had a basis of $80,000. The value of the house at the time of the donation was $250,000, and it had a $110,000 mortgage balance. How much gain must Larry realize when the gift is complete?

   A. $30,000
   B. $140,000
   C. $170,000
   D. $190,000

50. Ted transferred 800 shares of Zeta stock to his son, Mitch, but retained the right to receive lifetime income from half of the shares. If the share price of Zeta stock was $8.50 on the date of Ted's death, what amount will be included in his gross estate?

   A. $0
   B. $3,400
   C. $5,100
   D. $6,800

51. Ron and Deb, a married couple, purchased their home 8 years ago for $420,000. The fair market value was $670,000 when Ron died earlier this year. If the home was held as community property, what is Deb's new basis?

   A. $335,000
   B. $420,000
   C. $545,000
   D. $670,000

52. Kevin and Jennifer, a married couple, own a vacation home with a basis of $280,000 that is held in joint tenancy. If Kevin dies when the house is valued at $350,000, what will be Jennifer's new basis?

   A. $140,000
   B. $175,000
   C. $315,000
   D. $350,000

53. Ben made a lifetime gift of property with a fair market value of $335,000. Ben's basis in the property was $190,000, and he paid gift tax of $44,000. What is the donee's basis in the property?

   A. $190,000
   B. $198,250
   C. $209,045
   D. $214,865

54. Frank purchased a house for $250,000 and claimed depreciation of $40,000 before giving it to his father, Earl. The house was worth $310,000 at the time of the transfer, and Frank did not pay gift tax. Ten months later, Earl died when the house was worth $320,000, and the property passed back to Frank. What is Frank's basis in the inherited property?

A. $210,000
B. $250,000
C. $310,000
D. $320,000

55. Which of the following formulas is used to calculate the taxable amount of a net gift?

A. Taxable amount of net gift = Gross amount of gift – Gift tax paid by donor
B. Taxable amount of net gift = Gross amount of gift – Gift tax paid by donee
C. Taxable amount of net gift = Gross amount of gift + Gift tax paid by donor
D. Taxable amount of net gift = Gross amount of gift + Gift tax paid by donee

The following information relates to questions 56 – 60.
Jeff's uncle, Roger, gave him property with a fair market value of $16,000. Roger's basis was $20,000.

56. If Jeff sells the property for $22,000, what is his basis?

A. $0
B. $16,000
C. $20,000
D. $22,000

57. If Jeff sells the property for $22,000, what gain or loss will he recognize?

A. $2,000 loss
B. $2,000 gain
C. $4,000 gain
D. No gain or loss will be recognized.

58. If Jeff sells the property for $13,000, what is his basis?

A. $0
B. $13,000
C. $16,000
D. $20,000

59. If Jeff sells the property for $13,000, what gain or loss will he recognize?

A. $3,000 loss
B. $5,000 loss
C. $7,000 loss
D. No gain or loss will be recognized.

60. If Jeff sells the property for $18,000, what gain or loss will he recognize?

A. $2,000 loss
B. $2,000 gain
C. $4,000 gain
D. No gain or loss will be recognized.

ANSWER KEY

1. B
Step 1: ($19 × 5) + ($20 × 3) = $155
Step 2: $155 / 8 = $19.38

2. D
In a joint tenancy between non-spouses, 100% of the property will be included in the gross estate of the decedent unless the survivor shows consideration furnished.

3. D
Direct charitable contributions can be made at death without limit.

4. B
Basis = $36,000 / 3 = $12,000
There is no step-up in basis for lifetime gifts.

5. B
For a charitable remainder trust, the payout rate stated in the trust cannot be less than 5% or more than 50% of the initial fair market value of the trust's assets.

6. B
A charitable remainder annuity trust (CRAT) can pay Tyler a fixed percentage of the initial fair market value of the trust. With a charitable remainder unitrust (CRUT), the annual payout would be based on the fair market value of the trust revalued annually.

7. C
Crummey powers provide a beneficiary with a right of withdrawal equal to the lesser of the amount of the gift tax annual exclusion or the value of the gift transferred. In this question, the value of the gift ($175,000) is greater than the gift tax annual exclusion ($15,000), so the withdrawal right is limited to $15,000.

8. C
Crummey powers provide a beneficiary with a right of withdrawal equal to the lesser of the amount of the gift tax annual exclusion or the value of the gift transferred. In this question, the value of the gift ($8,000) is less than the gift tax annual exclusion ($15,000), so the withdrawal right is limited to $8,000.

9. C
Annaliese's stock receives a full step-up in basis at her death. Therefore, the basis will be $55 per share in the hands of her beneficiaries.

10. B
$2,000,000 × 0.35 = $700,000
To qualify for the Section 6166 election, a decedent's gross estate must include an interest in a closely-held business that exceeds 35% of the value of his or her adjusted gross estate.

11. A

$4,000	Checking account
+ $55,000	Savings account
+ $150,000	½ Value mutual fund
+ $395,000	Common stocks
+ $275,000	401(k)
+ $140,000	½ House
+ $28,000	½ Personal property
+ $31,000	½ Cars
$1,078,000	

12. B

For property owned joint tenants with rights of survivorship between spouses, 50% of the property will be included in the decedent's gross estate regardless of contribution.

13. D

For property owned joint tenants with rights of survivorship between non-spouses, 100% of the property will be included in the decedent's gross estate unless the survivor can prove that he or she made a contribution.

14. A

$3,000,000 \times 0.25 = \$750,000$

To qualify for the Section 2032A "special use valuation," the net value of real property used in a family farming operation must be at least 25% of the adjusted value of the decedent's gross estate.

15. D

$1,500,000 \times 0.5 = \$750,000$

To qualify for the Section 2032A "special use valuation," the net value of real and personal property used in a family farming operation must be at least 50% of the adjusted value of the decedent's gross estate.

16. D

The maximum reduction permitted to a decedent's gross estate under Section 2032A is $1,140,000 in 2018.

17. B

For community property, 50% of the property's value will be included in the decedent's gross estate regardless of contribution.

18. B

For property owned tenancy by entirety, 50% of the property will be included in the decedent's gross estate regardless of contribution.

19. D

For property held as tenancy in common, fractional ownership of the property is included in the decedent's gross estate.

20. C

$3,400,000	Gross estate
− $800,000	Debts
− $10,000	Funeral expenses
− $30,000	Casualty and theft losses
− $45,000	State death tax
$2,515,000	Adjusted gross estate

21. B

$3,400,000	Gross estate
− $800,000	Debts
− $10,000	Funeral expenses
− $30,000	Casualty and theft losses
− $45,000	State death tax
$2,515,000	Adjusted gross estate
− $800,000	Marital deduction
− $650,000	Charitable deduction
$1,065,000	Taxable estate

22. A
Taxable estate + Adjusted taxable gifts = Tentative tax base

23. D
Net estate tax + GSTT = Total estate tax

24. C
Tentative tax base × Estate tax rate = Tentative tax

25. C
To qualify for the Section 303 redemption, the stock's value must exceed 35% of the decedent's adjusted gross estate.

26. B
For a charitable remainder trust, the present value of the remainder interest that passes to charity must be at least 10% of the value of the property placed in the trust.

27. A
Because Karen has not gifted more than the unified credit amount of $5,600,000, she will not owe any gift taxes in 2018.

28. D
$5,600,000 + $5,600,00 + $15,000 + $15,000 = $11,230,000
Mary and Steve are each entitled to a unified credit of $5,600,000 in 2018. They can also each use their annual exclusion of $15,000.

29. C
Step 1: Bill's basis = ($44,000 / $57,300) × $44,000 = $33,787.09
Step 2: Bill's taxable gain = $44,000 − $33,787.09 = $10,212.91

30. D
At George's death, his daughter will not be able to prove any contribution because she has no records related to the purchase. Therefore, the full value of the condo on the date of death will be included in George's gross estate.

31. D
Since Louis did not outlive the term of the qualified personal resident trust (QPRT), the full value of the house on the date of death will be included in his gross estate.

32. C
$350,000 × 0.5 = $175,000
For married taxpayers, 50% of the value of property owned in joint tenancy is included in the gross estate, regardless of contribution.

33. C
Alison's basis = ($230,000 × 0.5) + ($350,000 × 0.5) = $290,000

34. C
$500,000 × 0.05 = $25,000
The greater of $5,000 or 5% of trust assets will be included in Jessica's gross estate. Therefore, $25,000 will be included.

35. D
Taxable gift = $93,000 – $15,000 = $78,000

36. B
Austin's basis of $47,000 carries over to his son, Jim, because this is a lifetime gift.

37. B
Taxable gain = $117,000 – $47,000 = $70,000

38. A
Taxable gift = $660,000 – $15,000 = $645,000

39. A
$660,000 – $600,000 = $60,000
If Robert sells the property for a loss, the basis is the lesser of the fair market value ($660,000) or the original basis ($1,200,000).

40. A
Because Tony has not gifted more than the unified credit amount of $5,600,000, he will not owe any gift taxes in 2018.

41. C
Taxable gift = $575,000 – $15,000 = $560,000

42. A
$600,000 × 0.5 = $300,000
For community property, 50% of the property's value will be included in the decedent's gross estate regardless of contribution.

43. D

Because the property was held as community property, Ruth receives a full step-up in basis at her husband's death.

44. B

Gift taxes paid are included in the gross estate of a donor for any taxable gifts made within 3 years of death. Therefore, $60,000 is included in Gretchen's gross estate.

45. A

If the transfer was made to Gretchen's husband instead of the trust, nothing would be included in her gross estate because the gift would qualify for the gift tax marital deduction.

46. A

Gifts of a future interest are not eligible for the gift tax annual exclusion.

47. C

Because there is no mention of the stock passing due to death, Tony's basis of $20,000 carries over to Charles and Jerry because these are lifetime gifts.

48. C

$320,000 \times 0.5 = $160,000$

For married taxpayers, 50% of the value of property owned in joint tenancy is included in the gross estate, regardless of contribution.

49. A

$110,000 – $80,000 = $30,000$

Larry's gain is the difference between the mortgage balance at the time of the transfer ($110,000) and his basis ($80,000).

50. B

Step 1: 800 shares $\times$ 0.5 = 400 shares
Step 2: 400 shares $\times$ $8.50 per share = $3,400

The value of 400 shares is included in Ted's gross estate because he retained the right to receive income from the shares for his life.

51. D

Because the home was held as community property, Deb receives a full step-up in basis at her husband's death.

52. C

Jennifer's basis = ($280,000 \times 0.5) + ($350,000 \times 0.5) = $315,000

53. C

Step 1: $44,000 \times [($335,000 – $190,000) / $335,000] = $19,045
Step 2: $19,045 + $190,000 = $209,045

54. A

$250,000 – $40,000 = $210,000

For a reverse gift, a step-up in basis is not allowed if the donee/decedent dies within one year of receiving a gift and then transfers the property back to the original donor. Frank must retain his original basis of $210,000.

55. B

Taxable amount of net gift = Gross amount of gift – Gift tax paid by donee

56. C

If Jeff sells the property for a gain, the original basis of $20,000 carries over from Roger.

57. B

$22,000 – $20,000 = $2,000 gain

58. C

If Jeff sells the property for a loss, the basis is the lesser of the fair market value ($16,000) or the original basis ($20,000).

59. A

$16,000 – $13,000 = $3,000 loss

60. D

For determining the gain, Jeff will use the carryover basis of $20,000. However, the property sold for $18,000 so there was no gain. Jeff will recognize no gain or loss on the transaction.

INDEX

Index

Made in the USA
Middletown, DE
04 December 2018